THE GENERALS ★ ★ ★ ★
AND THE ADMIRALS

Some Leaders of the United States Forces in World War II

THE GENERALS ★★★★
AND THE ADMIRALS

Some Leaders of the United States Forces in World War II

Portraits By T. H. CHAMBERLAIN

BIOGRAPHIES BY THE EDITORS OF *NEWSWEEK*

Essay Index Reprint Series

BOOKS FOR LIBRARIES PRESS
FREEPORT, NEW YORK

INTERNATIONAL STANDARD BOOK NUMBER:
0-8369-2362-6

LIBRARY OF CONGRESS CATALOG CARD NUMBER:
78-156646

PRINTED IN THE UNITED STATES OF AMERICA

P R E F A C E

THE BIOGRAPHIES IN THIS BOOK ARE DESIGNED TO SUPPLE-MENT PORTRAITS BY THE ARTIST. Source material from the files of NEWS-WEEK was checked against official biographies and all other available data by the research staff of the magazine, under the supervision of Lillian Chiriaka. All dates, promotions and incidents have been carefully checked against official data.

The author wishes to thank the officers and men of the Army, Navy, Marine and Coast Guard public relations offices for their prompt and willing answers to our many inquiries.

In a book of this size the absolute limit was thirty portraits. Naturally, there will be difference of opinion as to those chosen over others that might have been chosen. Present tables of organization would require a book at least four times as large were all three, four and five star officers to be included. And so, as a compromise, it was felt best to choose individuals who in general had, up to publication date, been most in the news reported from the fighting fronts. A second volume is in preparation.

To NEWSWEEK's managing editor Chet Shaw and associate editor Harry Kern must go a vote of thanks for their wholehearted cooperation in seeing this project through.

MARC R. FORE

January 1945

GENERAL GEORGE CATLETT MARSHALL

UNITED STATES ARMY

"We must make this war so terrible to the enemy, so overwhelming in character, that never again can a small group of dictators find sufficient following to destroy the peaceful security of the civilized world." . . . General Marshall. In spite of his lifetime of military training the General has maintained the attitude of the ordinary citizen, feeling that the Army should remain the servant of the people, and not become a dominant military caste.

George Catlett Marshall was born in Uniontown, Pennsylvania, Dec. 31, 1880, into a moderately wealthy and cultured family. Due to political differences he failed to obtain an appointment to the U.S. Military Academy, and so enrolled in Virginia Military Institute. In his freshman year at the military school he became a parade ground hero when, seriously wounded by a bayonet during a hazing stunt, young Marshall refused to say how the accident had happened or name the cadets involved. At the time of his graduation he was Senior First Captain and a recognized leader.

A short time after he obtained his second lieutenant's commission, Marshall married Elizabeth Carter Coles. Childless, she died in 1927.

Until 1907, Lieutenant Marshall served several tours of duty on the Pacific Coast, and in the Philippines. He was then sent to the Infantry-Cavalry School and the Army Staff College at Fort Leavenworth. This was an important step in his career. Efforts at energizing the Staff Command were just beginning and Marshall was just the sort of material they were looking for. He was graduated at the head of his class in 1908 and was immediately made an instructor. About this time he came to the attention of John J. Pershing. When the United States entered the war in 1917 Pershing sent Marshall, then a captain, to France ahead of most of the troops to study the war at first hand. Under fire he acquired the Croix de Guerre and the Legion of Honor. He was promoted to major. The following year he became a lieutenant colonel and Assistant Chief of Staff of the First Division. Pershing later made him operations head of the First American Army and Marshall distinguished himself by supervising the moving of fifteen divisions (nine in the line and six in reserve) of American troops into the Meuse-Argonne replacing the French divisions. This operation, conducted at night, in about two weeks, involved over 500,000 men, 27,000 guns, and mountains of food and supplies. Premature discovery by the enemy would have been disastrous. The entire maneuver was accomplished, and on September 6, 1918, the famous Argonne Offensive, destined to break the back of German resistance, began.

After the war, Marshall resumed his peacetime Army career and permanent rank of captain. Pershing, always an admirer, kept him on his staff as an aide for the next five years, a position allowing him to observe the inner workings of an Army command. Marshall was stationed in Tientsin, China, for three years before he became Assistant Commandant, Fort Benning, Georgia, where he helped reorganize the Infantry School. In 1930 he married Mrs. Katherine Boyce Tupper Brown of Baltimore and acquired three step-children.

He was detailed as Senior Instructor to the Illinois National Guard when he was finally made a colonel. Three years later, in 1936, he became Brigadier General Marshall.

In 1937, with war clouds gathering over the world, the United States renewed its interest in the Army. During efforts to revitalize the high command, Marshall was made Assistant Chief of Staff in the War Plans Division of the General Staff.

In the spring of 1939 General Malin Craig, scheduled for retirement, took a leave of absence and President Roosevelt appointed Marshall, who had been serving as Deputy Chief of Staff, as titular head of the Army. This was a jump over the heads of some thirty generals who held higher seniority ratings. The selection met with general acclaim from most of the senior officers. From his retirement General Pershing issued a statement that Marshall was the best possible selection. He was appointed Chief of Staff with the rank of general on September 1, 1939, and on December 15, 1944 was promoted to the newly created rank of General of the Army.

As Chief of Staff of an army of more than 7,500,000 of his fellow citizens engaged in the greatest military struggle in all history, George Catlett Marshall is filling a job for which he has trained himself for over 40 years.

T. H. Chamberlain.

GENERAL DOUGLAS MacARTHUR

UNITED STATES ARMY

By a strange twist of destiny, two generations of MacArthurs have been linked with the history of the Philippines. General Douglas MacArthur, whose gallant defense of the Bataan Peninsula won him the Congressional Medal of Honor in 1942, is the son of General Arthur MacArthur, Civil War hero, brigade commander at the capture of Manila in 1898, and later military governor of the Philippines.

Douglas MacArthur was born in Little Rock, Arkansas, January 26, 1880, the son of Arthur and Mary Pinkney MacArthur. After attending grade schools and the West Texas Military Academy he was appointed to West Point in 1899. His scholastic standing was very high and he was graduated with honors as First Officer of Cadets on June 11, 1903.

Young MacArthur was made a second lieutenant of engineers and assigned to the Philippines, where he remained until October, 1904. He spent a year in San Francisco before being ordered to Tokyo as aide to his father, General Arthur MacArthur.

Back once again in the States, Douglas was detailed as military aide to President Theodore Roosevelt in Washington. Later he attended the Engineer School of Application and, graduating in 1908, served in posts at Milwaukee, Fort Leavenworth, and San Antonio. In 1912 he was on detached duty in the Canal Zone. From November, 1912 to September, 1917, MacArthur filled varied routine details in Washington before accompanying the Vera Cruz expedition as assistant to the engineer officer.

During the last war Douglas MacArthur, at 37, was made Chief of Staff of the Rainbow Division and sailed with them to France in October, 1917. MacArthur was given command of the 84th Brigade and led it through offensives in St. Mihiel, Meuse-Argonne and Sedan. He was twice wounded in action. During the final phase of the war just prior to the Armistice, MacArthur achieved the dubious distinction of being taken prisoner by a patrol from the First Division, who mistook him for a German officer in the darkness and confusion.

MacArthur commanded the 84th Infantry Brigade with the Army of Occupation until April, 1919, when he returned to the U. S. to serve in the office of the Chief of Staff until June. He was Superintendent of the Military Academy at West Point for the next three years, the youngest man to hold that post. MacArthur was ordered to the Philippines where he served until 1925. Back in the U. S. again he became commander of the 4th Corps in Atlanta, and later the 3rd Corps, in Baltimore, until September, 1928. In that year he took the American Olympic Team, as its president, to the games at Amsterdam, Holland.

After his return from the Olympics, MacArthur was ordered to the Philippines as commander of the Manila district and later as commander of the entire Philippine Department. In September, 1930, he was detailed to command the 9th Corps in San Francisco. A month later, President Hoover, skipping many senior officers, selected Douglas MacArthur as Chief of Staff of the Army. With the rank of general, at the age of 50, he was the youngest officer ever to hold the position. MacArthur constantly struggled against the economy wave that gripped the nation, choking off army appropriations. He introduced the four-army defense system and fought for a larger air corps, tank and armored divisions.

MacArthur retired as Chief of Staff in October, 1935, to become Military Advisor to the Philippine Government. His good friend President Manuel Quezon made him Field Marshal of the Philippines and he labored long and hard at the task of making the island "impregnable." In July, 1941, President Roosevelt designated MacArthur Commanding General of the Far East Command. In December of that year came the tragic struggle on Bataan and Corregidor. General MacArthur was ordered to Australia and after a dramatic escape by boat and plane he assumed command of the combined U. S. Forces in the Southwest Pacific Area to start the long push back to the Philippines.

In December, 1944, MacArthur was given the new 5-star rank of General of the Army.

The General is deeply conscious of his self-imposed duty to the people of the Philippines, and says: "I was the leader of that lost cause and, from the bottom of my stricken heart, I pray that a merciful God may not delay too long their redemption, that the day of their salvation may not be so far removed that they perish . . ."

GENERAL DWIGHT DAVID EISENHOWER

UNITED STATES ARMY

The North African invasion required the utmost cooperation from all the forces involved. Dwight David Eisenhower, a lieutenant general, was chosen to command the conglomerate mass of armed might, French, British, United States and other Allied forces, as the war rolled along the southern shores of the Mediterranean, a region of varied religious and racial groups. Later, General Ike led another invasion, this time the main drive across the English Channel. He was named Supreme Commander of the Western Front and promoted to general.

David Dwight Eisenhower was born in Denison, Texas, October 14, 1890. Sometime during his childhood his given names were transposed and he became Dwight David Eisenhower. His birthplace has sometimes been given as Tyler, Texas, but the family Bible, West Point records, and his mother, who should know, all name Denison. The general's father, David Jacob Eisenhower, moved his family to Texas, where Dwight was born, and two years later moved back to Abilene, Kansas.

Dwight and his five brothers grew up as normal Midwestern boys, playing baseball and football, swimming in the near-by creek, and working in the creamery where the father was employed. All the Eisenhower boys were called Ike by their friends with appropriate added names such as Big Ike, Little Ike, Red Ike, and so on. Dwight was known as Ugly Ike, much to his mother's dismay.

After graduating from high school Dwight worked in and near Abilene for two years before entering West Point in 1911. He had intended going to Annapolis but found too late that he was slightly over the age limit for midshipmen.

At the Military Academy he was an average student, his grades placing him just above the middle of the class. He played on the football team until his knee was broken in a game with Tufts College. A typical cadet, he collected the usual demerits and was barred from school dances for a month for doing a fox-trot instead of the sedate two-step prescribed by authorities.

Eisenhower was graduated and commissioned a second lieutenant in 1915. During the last war he remained in the United States where he organized the Sixty-fifth Battalion of Engineers and later commanded Camp Colt, Pennsylvania, and a tank corps at Camp Dix, New Jersey.

He was later assigned to the Philippines at the request of General MacArthur, an admirer of his. He aided in organizing the defence of the Philippines and while there learned to fly.

When the United States entered the present war, Eisenhower was one of thousands of colonels in the service. However, Ike was one of the marked men in the Army, catalogued as good staff material. During the Louisiana maneuvers in the fall of 1941, he continued his brilliant record under General McNair, confirming his superiors' opinion of him. When the time came for the Allies to choose a Supreme Commander for the Western Front, Eisenhower was the obvious selection. Quite a tribute to his likable personality from the British. In England Eisenhower did everything possible to keep down friction between various nationalities. He issued an order stating that no remarks derogatory to any of the Allies would be tolerated, and on the lighter side, put up a penalty box in which men on the U. S. Headquarters Staff slipping into British mannerisms such as saying "rah-lly" had to drop a coin for each offence.

As Supreme Commander, Eisenhower controls the entire Western Front in Europe, Iceland, and the Mediterranean battle areas, territory he had studied after the last war. He was given a promotion to the new 5-star rank of General of the Army in December, 1944.

General Eisenhower is usually considered as rather gentle. When conditions warrant he can and does sound like a roaring bull. He is rather tall (6 feet), bald, blue-eyed, and has a smile which his wife, the former Marie Geneva Doud, describes as "wonderful." They have a son who was graduated from West Point in June 1944.

The general is a good bridge player, treating cards the way he does everything else, putting all the concentrated power he can muster on the job of the moment. In his moments of relaxation he reads all kinds of books and magazines with a special emphasis on military history.

GENERAL HENRY HARLEY ARNOLD

UNITED STATES ARMY

In 1910 a crude biplane fluttered to the grounds of the military post on Governors' Island, New York, and from it stepped the famous aeronaut, Glenn Curtiss, finishing a world's record flight—142 miles —all the way from Albany. Among the awed watchers at the finish line was a young second lieutenant of infantry named Henry H. Arnold. He determined from that moment to learn to fly.

Arnold applied for a change and, after being transferred to the Army Signal Corps, he was sent to Dayton, Ohio, for instruction in handling the Wright biplane. Two months later Arnold, back East, was training students at a newly-opened flight school on a tract of leased land near College Park, Maryland. In the fall of 1911 the school was moved to Augusta, Georgia, and young Arnold went along.

With the coming of warm weather in the spring, the College Park school was reopened and soon Arnold was back giving flight instruction. In the summer of 1912 he established a new altitude record by piloting a Burgess-Wright plane to the dizzy height of 6,540 feet.

The first Mackay Trophy to be awarded was won by Arnold, flying an early type Wright biplane over a fixed course from the College Park field to Fort Myer, Virginia, across the Potomac, and return. Even in those days, Arnold had a lot of color and the newspapers played up stories of the intrepid aviator who broke records and experimented with a mail-carrying scheme. He was the first military aviator to use radio in a plane for spotting artillery observations.

General Arnold was born in Gladwyne, Pennsylvania, June 25, 1886, the son of a doctor. An appointment to West Point was secured for his older brother, who decided not to use it. Henry took the examination instead and entered the Military Academy in the Class of 1907 whose members promptly named him Hap because of his constant grin.

Graduating, he served as an infantry second lieutenant in the Philippines. After he became an aviator he was sent to the Panama Canal Zone to organize an aviation service there. With the entry of the United States into the war in 1917, Arnold was brought to Washington and placed in charge of the Information Service of the Signal Corps Aviation Division. From there he went to the newly-formed Office of the Director of Military Aeronautics.

Advanced to the rank of colonel, Arnold made an inspection tour of aviation activities in France late in 1918. Back again in the United States, various commands in the new Air Service kept him busy on the Pacific coast until 1924. During this period Arnold assisted in projecting several Air Corps activities, among them the forest area patrol and experiments with refueling planes in the air.

Arnold's leadership of the Army Air Corps Alaskan Flight resulted in his winning the Mackay Trophy again in 1934. Hap really began his climb to the top of the rapidly expanding Air Corps in 1936 when he was appointed assistant to the Chief of the Air Corps. By June 1941 he had become Chief of Army Air Forces, retaining his duties as Deputy Chief of Staff for Air.

When the War Department General Staff was reorganized, Arnold became Commanding General of the Army Air Forces.

General Arnold is one of the first three army officers to become aviators and in a branch of the service where the seniority rule has little application, the fact that he is top man becomes doubly impressive. Many an oldtime flier with a record in the last war is serving in 1944 under a youngster only a few years out of West Point.

Back in the days when Gen. Billy Mitchell was predicting that airplanes could sink ships, to the scandal of battleship men, Arnold just escaped banishment along with the General. He was removed from the scene in Washington and sent to the field for a while to cool off.

In October 1944, Gen. Hap Arnold announced proudly for all the world to hear that his Army Air Force had dropped the total of a million tons of bombs on Axis targets and the guns of his fliers had destroyed 27,000 enemy planes.

On December 15, 1944, the Senate unanimously approved the President's nomination, promoting General Arnold to the new 5-star rank of General of the Army.

T.H.Chamberlain

GENERAL JOSEPH WARREN STILWELL

UNITED STATES ARMY

General Stilwell's nickname, Vinegar Joe, is supposed to have had its beginning at Fort Benning in 1929. Stilwell, a lieutenant colonel, was an instructor in infantry tactics. He felt called upon to give a hapless lieutenant a severe dressing down. The young officer pinned a cartoon on the bulletin board showing Stilwell's head outlined in a jug labeled vinegar. Stilwell thought it so funny he still keeps a copy.

The Stilwell family had lived in Yonkers, New York, for generations but Joseph Warren Stilwell was born in Palatka, Florida, March 19, 1883. Warren, as his parents called him, went to school in Yonkers and in Great Barrington, Massachusetts, where the family had a summer home. Reputedly to keep his rowdy son under control, the elder Stilwell got his friend, President McKinley, to give the boy an appointment to West Point. Entering the Academy in 1901, the future general found the military life much to his liking. By the time he was graduated, Stilwell stood 32nd in a class of 124. His athletic prowess and bad puns left a lasting memory.

With his commission as a second lieutenant tucked away, Stilwell married Winifred Smith of Syracuse, New York. She had been introduced to him by his sister, who had met the future Mrs. Stilwell at school.

Lieutenant Stilwell's first tour consisted of two years in the Philippines. During this time his desire to learn more of the Chinese people was awakened. Returning to the United States, Stilwell spent the next four years teaching at West Point. Transferred again to the Philippines, he served there another year, followed by a year at an Army post in Monterey, before settling down at the Academy for another four-year stretch.

After this country's entry into the war in 1917, Stilwell, promoted to major, reported to Camp Lee, Virginia. By December he was on his way overseas as a member of the American Expeditionary Forces. In France he was attached as observer, first to the British 58th Division, then to the French Seventeenth Corps. By September 1918, he was a lieutenant colonel and Assistant Chief of Staff for the Fourth Army Corps. He participated in engagements fought by the Corps at Verdun and St. Mihiel for which he was awarded the Distinguished Service Medal. After the armistice he entered Germany with the occupation troops. Finding his staff car repeatedly blocked by German civilians in cars, Stilwell sent an aide ahead in a motorcycle sidecar with a baseball bat. After a number of dented fenders and some glass broken, the Germans got the idea and kept out of Stilwell's way.

Back in the United States after the war, Stilwell began studying Chinese at the University of California, and then was detailed to the Orient for three years of duty at the American Embassy in Pekin, China.

In 1925 Stilwell returned to the United States and served at Fort Benning as assistant executive of the school there. He attended the important Command and General Staff School at Fort Leavenworth, before he was ordered back to China in August 1926. Two years later he was made Chief of Staff of American Forces in China. He was lent to the Chinese Government as the boss of a highway development employing over 12,000 coolies. It was during this period that Stilwell came to know Chiang Kai-shek and other Chinese leaders.

From 1929 till the summer of 1932, Stilwell was in several posts in the United States. Then came another long stay in China, from 1932 to 1939. During this time he arrived at his present opinion regarding the Japanese.

Fort Sam Houston, Texas, was Stilwell's next stop where he was in command of the Third Infantry Brigade, with the rank of brigadier general. On July 10, 1940, he took command of the Seventh Division in California, and in October, was promoted to major general.

With his extensive and specialized knowledge Stilwell was a natural choice of the President for a Chinese mission as Chief of Staff under Generalissimo Chiang Kai-shek. Uncle Joe took a plane and went back to China as a lieutenant general. Before his return to the United States in November, 1944, Stilwell was promoted to general.

T. H. Chamberlain

LIEUTENANT GENERAL BEN LEAR

UNITED STATES ARMY

After the 1941 maneuvers were over and the trucks were rolling back to their bases, one of them came to a halt on a hot, dusty road near Memphis, Tennessee. Sighting some shorts-clad girls on the golf course nearby, soldiers in the truck shouted, "Yoo-hoo!" To a male golfer who protested they said, "Hey, buddy, do you need a caddy?" "Buddy" turned out to be a wolf in civilian clothing—Lt. Gen. Ben Lear.

The general promptly turned the column of 350 men around and sent them back over their just completed maneuver in an attempt to instill a little discipline. This was the "incident" that had repercussions in Congress for some time. Two years later the nomination giving Lear permanent rank as lieutenant general was held up for a time because of feeling about the "Yoo-hoo" affair.

Ben Lear was born in Hamilton, Ontario, in 1879. Shortly afterwards his father moved to the United States. Ben followed his father's trade as a printer. Before the outbreak of the Spanish-American War in 1898 the elder Lear was in charge of the composing room of a newspaper in Pueblo, Colorado, with his son working for him. When the Colorado National Guard was mobilized, young Ben, a sergeant, was lining up the men for embarkation when he noticed a familiar figure. It was his father. Both of them were mustered out together in 1901. The younger Lear had seen extensive action in the Spanish-American War and in the Philippine Insurrection.

Taking advantage of an offer of a cavalry second lieutenant's commission in the Regular Army, Ben Jr. reenlisted and quickly made a reputation as a fearless rider and a first class shot. He served tours of duty at several posts in the United States and, shortly after marrying Grace Russel of Breckenridge, Missouri, left for service in Cuba. Returning to this country in 1909 Lear was sent to the crack cavalry station at Fort Myer, just across the Potomac from Washington, D. C.

The cavalry was a tough outfit and Ben Lear Jr. loved it. In those days the supreme test of an officer's caliber was how far and fast he could ride and how well he could shoot. Lear was rated a topnotcher.

A year later he was attending the Mounted Service School at Fort Riley, Kansas, and was made instructor of a training school for Army horse-shoers.

At the Olympic Games in Stockholm in 1912 Lear was one of the Army representatives in the rifle contests. Riding and shooting had always been a passion with him until he took up golf in recent years. He plays the game just as hard as he works on military problems.

The last war found Lear in the Army Service School at Fort Leavenworth and then he served eleven months with the General Staff in Washington.

By 1920 he had been promoted to lieutenant colonel and was Director of Horsemanship at Fort Riley Cavalry School. After two years Lear was ordered to the School of the Line at Fort Leavenworth. Upon graduation from the General Staff School and the Army War College he commanded a squadron of the Fourteenth Cavalry at Fort Sheridan, Illinois.

Next came a tour of duty with the Inspector General's office and then he became Commander at the Presidio, Monterey, California. After nearly two years as Chief of Staff of the Ninth Corps Area, he held his last Cavalry command at Fort Bliss, Texas.

Lear's next position was commander of the Pacific Sector of the Canal Zone defences. Now a major general, he remained in this important post for the next two years. Temporarily promoted to lieutenant general, he returned to the States in October 1940, and took command of the Second Army. Officers under his command point with pride to the fact that in less than a year's time, Lear assembled an entire army of some 125,000 men, trained them, and took them in field maneuvers through several Southern states in training combat with other groups. In July 1944, he became Commanding General, Army Ground Forces at Headquarters in Washington.

Lieutenant General Lear is a stickler for discipline. One of his maxims is, "Never let a mistake go uncorrected." He explains, "there are too many officers in the Army who are afraid of hurting someone's feelings."

LIEUTENANT GENERAL WALTER KRUEGER

UNITED STATES ARMY

Back in the stirring days of 1898, during the Spanish-American War, the Sixth United States Infantry marched through the streets of Cincinnati, Ohio. Among the spectators lining the curbs were two young men named Beckman and Krueger. Slapping Krueger on the back, Beckman said, "How would you like to be the colonel of that outfit?" Thirty-four years later, newly-promoted Colonel Krueger took command of the Sixth United States Infantry at Jefferson Barracks, Missouri.

Walter Krueger was born in Flatow, West Prussia, the son of Julius and Anna Krueger, January 26, 1881. His father died and his mother brought him to America when he was eight. They lived with her uncle, a prominent St. Louis resident, for a time.

In 1890 Mrs. Krueger remarried and the family moved to Stone Church, Illinois. Young Krueger attended public schools in the middle west. Another move saw the family in Madison, Indiana, where the future general went to high school. He later studied at Cincinnati Technical School.

Krueger volunteered for service in the Spanish-American War and was sent to Cuba. He served as a noncommissioned officer until he was mustered out in February 1899. By June he had seen enough of civilian life and reenlisted. Ordered to the Philippines, he fought as private, corporal, and sergeant with the Twelfth Infantry, seeing action in numerous engagements during the Philippine Insurrection on Luzon. On February 2, 1901, he was made a second lieutenant of infantry in the Regular Army, serving in the Islands until 1903.

Sent to the Infantry and Cavalry School at Fort Leavenworth, Krueger was graduated with distinction in August 1906 and was promoted to first lieutenant. He remained at Leavenworth as a student in the Staff College until 1907. Then, with the Twenty-third Infantry, he returned to the Philippines and took over a mapping detail in the central valley of the Island of Luzon.

In the United States again in 1909, Lieutenant Krueger became an instructor at Fort Leavenworth. Next he commanded a company at Madison Barracks, New York, until October, 1914, when he was assigned as Inspector in the Pennsylvania National Guard. When the guard was mobilized and sent to the Mexican border in 1916 he became a lieutenant colonel in the Tenth Pennsylvania Infantry.

Back in the Regular Army again as a captain, he was ordered to Washington in June 1917 for duties at the Militia Bureau. While there he planned the overseas service organization for the National Guard. Later that year he was Acting Chief of Staff of the 84th Division.

Sent to France in February 1918, he was immediately placed in the Staff College at Langres. In June he was made Assistant Chief of Staff of the 26th Division for one month. He returned to the United States and took a similar job with the 84th Division in Ohio. Now a lieutenant colonel, Krueger shuttled back to France with that division and remained with it until October when he was detailed as a Chief of the Tank Corps, AEF, with headquarters at Chaumont.

After the armistice was signed, Krueger served as instructor at Langres until January 1919. Later he was made Assistant Chief of Staff of the Fourth Army Corps stationed in Cochem, Germany.

A temporary colonel at the war's end, Krueger reverted to his permanent rank, captain, in June 1920. In less than a year he became a lieutenant colonel (permanent) and in 1922 he was sent to Germany to study secret war archives and documents. Domestic assignments in the War Plans Division of the General Staff and on the Joint Planning Board of the Army and Navy followed.

Next he spent eight months at flying school and in early 1928 Krueger went to the Naval War College for a four-year period as a member of the staff. Because of that service and his many cruises with the Fleet while on the General Staff, Krueger probably knows more high naval officers than anyone else in the Army.

He was made brigadier general in October 1936 and in the spring of 1941 he was assigned to command the Third Army in San Antonio, Texas, and was promoted to lieutenant general (temporary). In February 1943 he assumed command of the Sixth Army in Australia. He was transferred at the particular request of General MacArthur, South Pacific Commander.

LIEUTENANT GENERAL BREHON BURKE SOMERVELL

UNITED STATES ARMY

"Just a country boy . . . trying to get along in the big city," is the way tall, dapper, grey-haired General Somervell describes himself. There seems to be little support for such a remark. He was born in Little Rock, Arkansas, May 9, 1892. His father, a doctor, was handicapped in his practice by deafness. So his mother, a spirited schoolteacher, took matters into her own hands, and moving to Washington, she started a girl's school known as Belcourt Seminary. It soon became popular and fashionable.

General Somervell resolutely denies spending much time around the school. He did remain in Washington long enough to finish two years of high school before attending a preparatory school at Cornwall, N. Y. Somervell had given some thought to entering Annapolis, but the sight of two resplendent West Pointers parading down the street during Christmas leave settled the matter.

His classmates at the Academy recall "Bill" Somervell as having been somewhat of a dandy. The school yearbook says, "A thoroughbred, clean cut—both externally and internally . . . if you could take Bill's mind out and examine it, you would find it pigeonholed and arranged like a card index." These qualities are even more in evidence today. Commissions in the Engineer Corps were much coveted by the cadets and the first fifteen in class standing were allowed their choice. Somervell stood sixth in a class of 106.

Second Lieutenant Somervell happened to be near Paris at the time of the war's outbreak in August 1914. Reporting at the Embassy, he was pressed into service doling out a million dollars in gold to stranded Americans. This was a forerunner of his many big spending jobs.

Back in the United States, after service in New England and Texas he was ordered to accompany General Pershing on the Punitive Expedition to Mexico. General Pershing put Somervell to work building and maintaining the expedition's supply roads. His superior officer said of him at the time, "Somervell is the best officer I ever saw, or hope to see."

After a term at the Engineer School, Washington, D. C., Somervell was promoted to captain, and helped to organize the Fifth Reserve Engineers.

They sailed for France in July 1917, as one of the first construction outfits to go abroad for the AEF. For over a year Bill Somervell faithfully supervised Army installations.

Growing more restless as 1918 wore on, he requested a transfer to the scene of action, but to no avail. When his leave finally came up, Somervell borrowed his commander's staff car and headed for the front.

A citation given to Somervell, together with the Distinguished Service Cross, tells the story of his venture. It reads, "Voluntarily serving on the staff of the 89th Division, he conducted the first engineering reconnaissance of the damaged bridges at Pouilly . . . advancing more than 500 meters beyond the American outposts, crossing three branches of the Meuse River and successfully encountering the enemy."

After the Armistice, Somervell was Assistant Chief of Staff in the Army of Occupation in Germany. In 1925, the Army granted him a leave of absence to assist in a survey of the Danube and the Rhine Rivers for the League of Nations.

In 1933 the Turkish Government requested the services of Somervell, and so he spent a year making an economic survey and covered thousands of miles of Turkish territory. Sometimes his car had to be ferried across streams by hand. When he turned in his massive reports, Turkish officials told him that he knew more about the country than any native.

In 1935, Somervell was manfully engaged in digging the ill-fated Florida Ship Canal when he was called to New York to unsnarl the gigantic WPA mess there. Supervising about 200,000 people he stuck to that job until 1940. When authorities had trouble housing the growing draft armies, Somervell was assigned to the Quartermaster Corps to build cantonments. His lack of regard for established rules is notable. "We have only one objective and we must evade, erase and knock out all rules, restrictions and habits that get in our way," he says. He won the respect of War Secretary Stimson, Under Secretary Patterson and General Marshall, and who saw to it that, when the Army Service Forces was organized, General Somervell was the man in charge.

T.H. Chamberlain

LIEUTENANT GENERAL JONATHAN MAYHEW WAINWRIGHT

UNITED STATES ARMY

Shortly before midnight on May 4, 1942, the first Japanese barges succeeded in landing on the shore at Corregidor Island. This was the beginning of the last phase of the conquest of the Philippines. Throughout the next day and into the dawn of the next the unequal struggle continued. The last communication to the War Department from the defenders came on May 6 and said that fighting had ceased and that terms of surrender were under discussion. The message was signed by Lt. Gen. Jonathan Wainwright, commander of American forces in the Philippines.

Offered an opportunity to escape to Australia with one of the last relief planes to leave the Rock, Wainwright said, "I have been with my men from the start, and if captured I will share their lot. We have been through so much together that my conscience would not let me leave before the final curtain . . ."

General Wainwright suffered the bitterest experience of a soldier's career when he was led away, first to Tarlac, north of Manila, and later to the Island of Formosa to while away the rest of the war in a prisoner-of-war camp.

Jonathan Wainwright was born in Walla Walla, Washington, August 23, 1883, at a time when the area was a territory and Indians were still on the warpath. His father was Major Robert P. Wainwright, who was graduated from West Point in 1875, and achieved distinction as an Indian fighter. The major obtained an appointment to the Military Academy from President Theodore Roosevelt for his son. At the Academy young Wainwright became an outstanding student. He was graduated in 1906 at the age of 22 with the highest military honor, that of "First Captain of the Corps of Cadets." He was a marksman, class toastmaster, and hop manager. The yearbook for his class says, "This is IT, the goal of every good cadet's ambition. Many honors have been heaped upon Skinny's head, so that it's a wonder that his slender frame has withstood their bending movement without any more damage than giving to his knees a permanent set."

After his graduation and commissioning as a second lieutenant, Wainwright was sent to duty in border cavalry camps until, with his regiment, he sailed for the Philippines in June 1909. He took part in an expedition against hostile tribes on the Island of Jolo. Back in the United States in February of 1910 he served with the First Cavalry at various posts and was a member of the Cavalry Rifle Team.

The Army sent Wainwright to the Mounted Service School for a special course and he returned to the First Cavalry. Among the posts he served in was the Presidio of San Francisco during the Panama-Pacific Exposition.

When the United States entered the last war, Wainwright was assigned to Plattsburg Barracks, New York, as Adjutant of the First Officers' Training Camp. From there he went to Camp Devens, Massachusetts, for duty with the General Staff of the Seventy-sixth Division, sailing for France with them early in 1918. Until June 1918 he was a student at the General Staff College at Langres. When he completed the course Wainwright was detailed to the Eighty-second Division and served with it during the St. Mihiel and Meuse-Argonne Offensives. After the Armistice, he served with the American forces in Germany at Coblenz until October 1920.

Back in the United States, Wainwright spent most of the time until 1928 with the War Department General Staff. Then he attended the Chemical Warfare School at Edgewood Arsenal, the advanced course at the Fort Riley Cavalry School, and the Command and General Staff School at Fort Leavenworth. In the summer of 1933 he was ordered to attend the Army War College in Washington.

Wainwright went to the Philippines in September 1940 and in October, promoted to major general, he assumed command of the Philippine Division. He took command of the entire Philippine Theater in the dark days of 1942 upon General MacArthur's transfer to Australia. He has been a prisoner of the Japanese since the surrender of Corregidor Fortress.

In August 1944 the International Red Cross said that one of their delegates had interviewed General Wainwright and that the general stated: ". . . conditions in Camp V were as good as can be reasonably expected."

LIEUTENANT GENERAL JOSEPH T. McNARNEY

UNITED STATES ARMY

Tall, lean, dark and taciturn, Joe McNarney is one of the youngest men ever to become Deputy Chief of Staff. He holds ratings as a Command Pilot, Combat Observer and Technical Observer. Usually, when travelling by plane, he takes over the controls. His friends say that his Scotch-Irish ancestry and upbringing wouldn't let him give a friend a break and, strange to say, they admire him for it. Fellow officers call him ruthless, but absolutely fair and objective.

Joseph McNarney was born in Emporium, Pennsylvania, on August 28, 1893. His father was an able lawyer and former public prosecuter, and his mother was an ardent temperance worker.

One of McNarney's early recollections is of his uncle, resplendant in his Army blues. Young Joe determined to wear a soldier's uniform and also to become an aviator. He was a rather shy lad during his school days in Emporium, and is remembered as being quite a bookworm.

Following his graduation from West Point, McNarney was commissioned a second lieutenant in June 1915, and was sent to the Twenty-first Infantry detachment at Vancouver Barracks, Washington. He was made a student instructor at the Signal Corps Aviation School at San Diego, California, completed his flying training and received a rating as Junior Military Aviator in April 1917. He was among the first fliers in the Army when the United States entered the last war. McNarney remained at the school as an instructor in Meteorology and Radio Telegraphy until May 1917.

While stationed in San Diego, Joe McNarney had met a young schoolteacher named Helen Wahrenberger. They were married in June, and in August he was ordered to France where he served with the First Aero Squadron at Etampes, Avord, and Amanty, and as Assistant Director of the First Corps Aeronautical School.

McNarney held several different posts in the next few months in command and headquarters assignments. He participated in the Château Thierry Offensive as Commander of Observation Group, First Corps, and on the staff of the Chief of Air Service of the First Army. He was respectively Commander of the Fourth and Fifth Corps Observation Groups during the St. Mihiel and Meuse-Argonne Offensives.

In the spring of 1919, McNarney assisted in the writing of a manual on Air Observation at Army headquarters in Paris. He returned to the United States that summer and was assigned the command of Godman Field, Fort Knox, Kentucky, until October, when he took command of the flying school at Gerstner Field, Lake Charles, Louisiana.

McNarney was then transferred to Langley Field, where he spent the next five years as instructor in the Field Officers' School, later named the Air Corps Tactical School.

In the fall of 1925 he was sent to the important Command and General Staff School at Fort Leavenworth for special training. In June 1926, he was graduated as an honor student. The next three years were spent at the War Department, Air Section, Military Intelligence Division, followed by a course in the Army War College. Following this McNarney was assigned several command posts in succession and then was ordered back to Washington as an instructor in the Army War College. From 1935 to 1938 he was Assistant Chief of Staff, G-4, Air Force General Headquarters. In the spring of 1939 he reported for duty with the War Plans Division of the General Staff, and a year later was appointed a member of the Permanent Joint Defense Board, Canada-United States.

McNarney was a member of the Special Observers Group sent to England during the blitz in the summer of 1941. The Japanese attack on Pearl Harbor brought him home in a hurry and he was promptly assigned as Air Forces representative on the Roberts Commission. McNarney carried out the much needed reorganization of the Army General Staff, sending some 500 officers into the field, from a total of 800. The General Staff had not been overhauled since its creation at the turn of the century, and was a maze of red tape and overlapping authorities. McNarney was just the man to do this job, most officers admitting that he is harsh, but just. He was made Deputy Chief of Staff of the United States Army in March 1942, and in October he was designated Deputy Supreme Allied Commander, in the Mediterranean Theater and Commanding General of United States Army Forces in that area.

LIEUTENANT GENERAL MARK WAYNE CLARK

UNITED STATES ARMY

One spot of cheer for the GI's slogging away on the Italian battle line, sometimes called the Forgotten Front, was the presence of Mark Wayne Clark, the general who "got lonesome" for his men and gave up a well-equipped palace belonging to a titled Neapolitan to go back to his office-home, truck headquarters in the field, to be with his soldiers.

His men like to be with him too, as the following note indicates: "We, the undersigned, would like to stay where General Clark stays, and move where he moves. In other words, we request assignment to duty right here." The "undersigned" were a group of colored aircraft gunners whom Clark had questioned about home and Army life a few days previously while they were on duty, protecting staff headquarters.

Although a firm believer in discipline, Clark is not regarded as a tough guy by his men. There is something about the tall, heavy-shouldered man that commands respect.

There is a lot about Clark's Army record to command respect too. He was the youngest man in the Army's history to receive the three stars of a lieutenant general. Clark was only 46 at the time. While he was serving in England as General Eisenhower's Deputy Commander, Clark was chosen to lead the secret mission to North Africa, to travel by plane, submarine and finally in rubber boats, and land and set up, under the noses of the Vichy French and Nazis, plans for the Allied invasion of Africa.

As the Deputy Commander in Chief of forces landing in North Africa, Clark saw at first hand the results of his undercover activities. For his work before and during the landings he was given the Distinguished Service Medal.

While in Africa with the Fifth Army he set up a rigorous battle training program for his troops, simulating actual fighting as nearly as possible, including the use of live ammunition to get the men used to battle conditions.

Later on General Clark led the invasion forces in the landings at the bloody beachhead of Salerno. Clark holds the Legion of Merit Award, received in 1943 for laying the groundwork in the housing and training program for American forces in the European theater.

He assumed command of the Fifth Army in January 1943, for the slow push up the Italian boot, and in November 1944, General Clark was made Commander of all Allied Armies in Italy.

An Army career was always the goal of Mark Wayne Clark. He was born at Madison Barracks, New York, on May 1, 1896, the son of Colonel C. C. Clark, post commander. He went to high school at Highland Park in Illinois. At West Point he was known as Wayne and was definitely not one of the scholars. He was 110th in a class of 139, with his best marks in history and philosophy. After his graduation in 1917, he served in the last war, and was wounded by shrapnel while leading his battalion in the Vosges sector of the French front.

Between wars he advanced from captain to brigadier general, skipping the grade of colonel on the way, carrying out a variety of assignments. Clark studied at Command and Staff School and the Army War College, becoming an instructor in the latter. In August of 1940, he was ordered to duty with the General Headquarters Staff, and was later made Deputy Chief of Staff under General McNair. In that post he helped the Army over growing pains incidental to its sudden wartime mushrooming growth.

General Clark says that he chose the infantry because "She is the Queen of Battles," and incidentally to follow in his father's footsteps. His son, William, a West Pointer, is carrying on the family tradition, making the fourth generation of Clarks to become Army officers.

General Clark married Maurine Doran of Muncie, Indiana, in 1924. The Clarks first met on a blind date in Washington. Later she was engaged to another officer but the competition spurred Clark into proposing to her while she was coming back from a trip to see his parents. Clark has always enjoyed family life, taking long walks with his children. After the war he wants to move to Puget Sound and devote himself to fishing. In spite of the general's engaging qualities, he is not fond of social functions and has little time for small talk.

T.H. Chamberlain

LIEUTENANT GENERAL GEORGE S. PATTON, JR.

UNITED STATES ARMY

A feature of the 1912 Olympic games held in Stockholm, Sweden, was the spectacular, mad, driving energy displayed by a young U.S. officer athlete. Reporters called him the "incredible" Patton. In the pentathlon competition he was the only foreign officer to give the Swedes any trouble. In the fencing matches he was described as showing, "unusual calm and calculation, skilfully exploiting his opponent's every weakness." In the target shoot, the officials failed to find one of Patton's shots. It had undoubtedly gone through another previous bullet hole in the paper, but it was counted as a miss. Even with this stroke of bad luck, Patton still finished fifth.

"Old Blood and Guts" Patton is still exploiting his opponent's every weakness, in his second world war. His dramatic successes in the African campaign, his rampaging tank race across France with his Third Army, and his hammering attack on the Siegfried Line are typical of the man. One of his battle orders read, "We shall attack, and attack, until we are exhausted, and then we shall attack again."

Patton was born on his father's ranch near San Gabriel, California, November 11, 1885. His parents were wealthy, fox-hunting aristocrats, originally from Virginia. He rode a great deal as a boy, and later at Virginia Military Institute became an expert polo player. At V.M.I. he is remembered mostly for his bizarre costumes and practical jokes. He played football and was a star performer on a horse.

He secured an appointment to West Point in 1904, and left V.M.I. With his tremendous athletic energy, and his faith in his destiny, Patton cut quite a swath at the Academy. He became so interested in cadet life that he spent five years instead of the usual four at the Point. In the process he did become class adjutant. A year after his graduation, Patton married Beatrice Ayer of Boston. Her family, also wealthy, had long been friends of the senior Pattons.

As was expected, Patton, a true blueblood, joined the cavalry. When he arrived at his post in Texas Patton astonished his fellow officers by turning up with a string of 23 polo ponies in tow. He was known as an expert with rifle, pistol and saber.

During the Mexican border trouble in 1916 Patton literally sat on General Pershing's doorstep in an effort to get sent into action. He was finally allowed to track down a particularly annoying bandit. After a wild-west chase and with his man barricaded behind some adobe walls, Patton rushed in with six-guns blazing and dramatically hove into sight shortly after with the bandit, dead, and draped across his shoulder, blanket fashion.

Soon after the U.S. entry into the war in 1917, it became evident that the cavalry was no place for a man of action. In one skirmish with the Germans Patton jumped from his stalled tank and with a few men charged the enemy on foot. In the exchange of shots most of the group were killed or wounded and Patton was hospitalized for the rest of the war. He came back to the United States a colonel, suitably decorated with the Distinguished Service Cross.

With the war out of the way, Patton studied all the military history he could find and kept to his rigid athletic program, certain that another war would come and sure that he would have his place in it.

On one of his tours of duty Patton was sent to Hawaii. He and his wife bought a small sailboat and made their way out to the Islands the hard way. Since then he has bought a larger boat, now in storage against the time he will be free to use it again.

At the time General Patton was detailed to the Armored Forces, he took a good deal of ribbing in the newspapers when he appeared in a dramatic outfit of his own design. It consisted of a green jacket with white buttons, trousers to match with black striping down the leg. This creation was topped off with a heavily padded crash helmet in gold. For a while after that episode he was known as "The Green Hornet." Fellow officers call him a modernized version of dashing Confederate General J. E. B. Stuart with a touch of General Nathan Bedford Forrest thrown in for generous good measure.

During the wild turmoil of the Battle of France, Patton bellowed to his Chief of Staff, "We are going to attain our objective even if you have to drive a tank and I have to to fire its guns." . . . and he meant it.

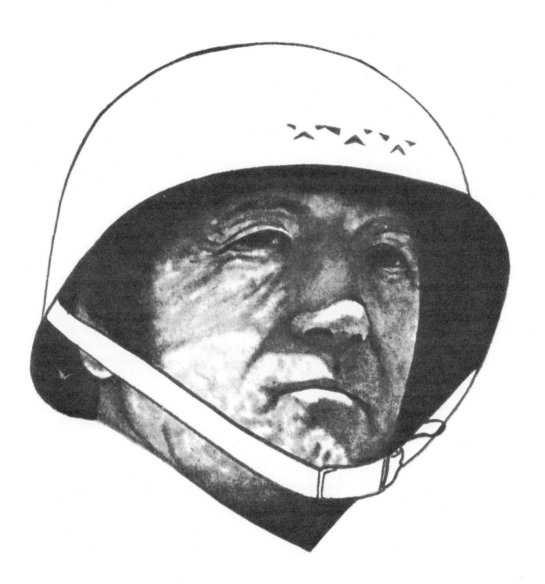

LIEUTENANT GENERAL CARL ANDREW SPAATZ

UNITED STATES ARMY

For weeks in the summer of 1940, a man in civilian dress, mustached, of medium height, sat and watched the progress of the German blitz over southern England. The man was Carl A. Spaatz, sent to Britain as an observer for the U.S. Air Corps. While looking on at the Nazis' supreme efforts he changed his mind about the invincibility of Goering's Luftwaffe. "The damn fools," he fumed, "they're setting air power back twenty years."

When Spaatz returned to the United States, he was placed in charge of the Matériel Division of the Air Corps. This assignment lasted until January 1942, when he was made Chief of the Air Force Combat Command. From there he was detailed to Headquarters, Army Air Forces, in Washington. In May 1942 he became Commanding General of the Eighth Air Force.

Spaatz went to Britain in July of 1942 with his command and moved on to North Africa, first in command of the Northwest African Air Forces; later as Commanding General of all U.S. Army Air Forces in that theater, in addition to his other duties. When General Eisenhower was realigning his high command in preparation for the invasion and liberation of France, Spaatz was given command of the U.S. Strategic Air Force in the European Theater of Operations. General Spaatz carries a rating as a Command Pilot and Combat Observer. Unofficially he is rated as a demon poker player, chain smoker and coffee drinker.

Carl Andrew Spaatz was born in Boyertown, Pennsylvania, on June 28, 1891, of German descent. He speaks the language fluently. Following his graduation from the Military Academy at West Point he became a second lieutenant of infantry, on June 12, 1914. His first station was Schofield Barracks, Hawaii. After a year in the islands he was sent to the Aviation School at San Diego, California.

Spaatz was ordered to France during the last war and assigned to the American Aviation School at Issoudun in France. He served there until August 1918, during which time the school grew from a few small buildings into one of the world's largest aviation schools of the period. He joined the Second Pursuit Group at the front in September, as a pilot.

Promoted to flight leader, he was officially credited with having shot down three Fokker planes in aerial combat during the St. Mihiel and Meuse-Argonne Offensives. He was awarded the Distinguished Service Cross for heroism in action.

After the war, Spaatz returned to America, early in 1919. He was placed in charge of an Army Flying Circus to publicize the Victory Loan Drive, in April 1919. In October he took part in a transcontinental reliability and endurance test from California to New York. He held various command posts until September 1924, when he was sent to the tactical school at Langley Field, Virginia, and upon graduating was assigned to Air Corps Headquarters in Washington.

In 1929, Carl Spaatz commanded the *Question Mark*, during its epochal refueling and endurance flight over Los Angeles. He kept the plane aloft for 150 hours, 50 minutes and 15 seconds. For this he was given the Distinguished Flying Cross. Following several routine duty tours for the next few years, Spaatz enrolled in the Command and General Staff School at Fort Leavenworth, and was graduated in June 1936. In 1939 he was in the Office of the Chief of Air Corps as Assistant Executive Officer. After this duty he was sent as observer to Britain in 1940.

One day at Langley Field, in 1937, General Spaatz's wife and two oldest daughters ganged up on him. Up until that time he had been using the name he had been born with, spelled Spatz and pronounced "Spotz". His family said that they were tired of being called "spats". They debated about changing it to "Spotz" when Mrs. Spaatz remembered that a Belgian branch of the family spelled it "Spaatz". They informed the general that henceforth he was to be known as General Spaatz.

When Carl Spaatz entered West Point in 1910, he was promptly dubbed, "Toohey," after an upperclassman, redheaded and freckled faced like himself. The nickname was later shortened to Tooey.

In October of 1944, General Spaatz was awarded the Oak Leaf Cluster to add to his previously won Distinguished Service Medal, for his efforts in command of two widely separated Air Forces in the strategic bombing of Nazi-dominated Europe.

LIEUTENANT GENERAL OMAR NELSON BRADLEY

UNITED STATES ARMY

"The Doughboy's General" is the label attached to Omar Bradley by the men under his command. He is invariably polite and considerate. During a particularly difficult interview with a surrendering German staff officer, one of Bradley's aides accidentally fired his carbine. The bullet sang past the general's ear. "Be more careful with that damn thing, please," he said.

In the Tunisian Campaign a German officer stiffly requested surrender terms. Bradley said, "My terms are unconditional surrender. There must be no sabotage of equipment, and no attempt to evacuate by sea. We will kill anyone who tries to get out." Then, in an aside to his aides, he remarked, "I guess I'm just old Unconditional Surrender Grant himself." At times he said that he would much rather be hunting wild boars than Germans.

General Bradley has long, strong legs on a lean athletic body. He stands as straight as a ramrod. His bushy, black eyebrows and piercing grey eyes peer from behind large tinted tortoise-shell glasses. He has a domelike forehead and grey-speckled hair, baldish on top. Bradley is generally recognized as a great tactician. He is slow spoken, but quick-witted, still retaining his Midwestern drawl.

Bradley's photographic memory and mathematical mind make him a first class bridge and poker player. He regularly takes part in a game that has lasted for twenty years or more with some of his cronies. He plays cards with shrewdness and enthusiasm. Baseball is his greatest love. As far back as his high school days Omar Bradley was a crack player. At West Point he was a noted star and still holds the Academy record for distance throwing. He also likes to hunt. In Missouri when Omar was a boy, his father used to take him on hunting trips. He likes plain food, steaks and ice cream.

Omar Nelson Bradley was born in Clark, Missouri, on Lincoln's birthday, February 12, 1893, the son of a school teacher. Bradley's father died when he was 13 and his mother moved to Moberly, Missouri, and remarried. He went to high school in Moberly, and after graduating, wrote a letter to his congressman asking for a West Point appointment. The congressman gave Bradley an alternate appointment, but the principal failed, and so Omar was admitted.

At the time of his graduation from West Point, the class yearbook had this to say: "His most prominent characteristic is getting there, and if he keeps up the clip he has started, some of us will be bragging to our grandchildren that "Sure, General Bradley was a classmate of mine." In keeping with the prophecy, Bradley was the first member of his class to reach the rank of general.

For several years after he graduated from the Academy, Bradley was assigned posts in the West, from Vancouver Barracks to the Mexican border. In December 1918, he was detailed to Camp Grant, Illinois. From there he went to South Dakota State College, as Professor of Military Science and Tactics. Then he was sent to West Point as mathematics instructor for four years. He was ordered to duty in Hawaii in the spring of 1925 and after holding several posts he returned to the United States in 1928.

Bradley went through the Command and General Staff School at Fort Leavenworth, and was graduated in July 1929. For the next four years he served as instructor at the Fort Benning Infantry School. He then entered the Army War College in Washington, and was graduated in June 1934, and then went back to West Point as an instructor.

In June of 1938, Bradley was called to Washington for duty on the War Department General Staff. When the officers' training center was expanded at Fort Benning, Bradley was detailed to run it. Within a short time he had quietly arranged the school so that it could handle 14,000 prospective officers at once. Bradley was commander of a division during the field maneuvers in Louisiana in 1942. After several other shifts in command posts, he was named Commanding General, Second Corps, in North Africa, as of May 1943.

He was assigned to the European Theater of Operations in September 1943, and on the following January, General Eisenhower, Allied Supreme Commander announced Bradley's appointment as a senior commander of American ground troops in the European area.

T.H. Chamberlain

LIEUTENANT GENERAL JAMES HAROLD DOOLITTLE

UNITED STATES ARMY AIR FORCES

The aircraft carrier *Hornet* turned into the wind; Admiral Mitscher wished the Army commander good luck, and medium bombers of the U. S. Army Air Forces began to take off for the 900-mile run to the Japanese mainland. The famous Tokyo Raid from Shangri-La was under way. The date was April 18, 1942, and the commander was Lt. Col. Doolittle.

James Harold Doolittle was born in Alameda, California, December 14, 1896. Shortly afterwards his parents took him to Nome, Alaska, returning when he was eleven. He had completed three years of study at the University of California when he enlisted in the Signal Corps Reserve as a flying cadet on October 6, 1917.

He was sent to the School of Military Aeronautics at the University and then went to Rockwell Field, California, for advanced training.

He was commissioned a first lieutenant in the Air Service, Regular Army, and in September of 1922, made the first of the cross-country flights that brought him international fame. He flew from Florida to California with one stop, and won the Distinguished Flying Cross.

In 1922 Doolittle was assigned to McCook Field, Ohio, for experimental work there. In 1923 he went to Massachusetts Institute of Technology for special courses and was graduated with the degree of Doctor of Science. In the late summer of 1925, Doolittle was attached to the Naval Air Station, in Washington, to take special training in flying high-speed seaplanes. He served with the Naval Test Board at Mitchel Field for a short period. This same year he won the Schneider Trophy Race, and the Mackay Trophy.

As a racing and test pilot, Doolittle also won the Bendix Trophy Race, the Thompson Trophy Race and numerous city-to-city speed races. He was the first pilot to fly across the continent in a single day, first to fly the dangerous outside loop, first to take off, fly a predetermined course and land without being able to see the ground, and first to get the speed of landplanes above 300 miles an hour. The Guggenheim Foundation obtained his services for their experiments in fog flying. This work is considered the greatest single step in air safety.

In April of 1926, Jimmy Doolittle was granted leave of absence to demonstrate planes in South America. While in Chile, at a party, he fell from a balcony while doing a handstand and broke both his ankles. The plane demonstrations had to go on, regardless, so Doolittle strapped his cast-enclosed feet to the rudder bars and flew his plane, using combat tactics and maneuvers. Later, still in his casts, with his crutches beside him, he flew across the Andes on his way home.

The Army Air Forces had built Jimmy a special plane for use in the 1929 Cleveland Air Races. He arrived the day of the show and took his plane out for a test flight. Coming down in a terrific power dive, the plane wings came off, with Doolittle right behind them in his parachute. Apparently nerveless, he showed up at the races, borrowed another plane and thrilled the crowd with another power dive.

On February 15, 1930, he resigned his commission in the Regular Army and accepted a commission as major in the Officers Reserve Corps. He made several experimental flights and was awarded the Harmon Trophy for his instrument flying tests. In 1934 he became a member of the Army board to study Air Corps Organization.

As a civilian, he won the Bendix Trophy Race from Burbank, California, to Cleveland, Ohio. In July 1940 he was ordered back into active duty. In the fall of that year he was assigned to Detroit to work with the conversion of automobile plants to airplane parts production. During this period he went to England for a short time as a member of a special mission. Promoted to lieutenant colonel, Doolittle was sent to Washington for a while before he started his Tokyo adventure in April 1942. For this intrepid flight he was awarded the Congressional Medal of Honor and made a brigadier general.

In September 1942 he was given command of the Twelfth Air Force in Africa. He was named commanding general of the Fifteenth Air Force in November 1943 and on January 1, 1944 he became commander of the Eighth Air Force in the European Theater of Operations. In March 1944, he was promoted to the grade of lieutenant general.

T.H. Chamberlain

ADMIRAL ERNEST JOSEPH KING

UNITED STATES NAVY

During the last war, Ernie King was a guest of Admiral Jellicoe aboard his flagship, observing the effects of a naval bombardment on German-held Ostend, Belgium. When an enemy shell landed close by, British Jellicoe quipped, "There's one to tell your grandchildren about." Said King, "The distance will get shorter with the years." King was aide and later Assistant Chief of Staff to Admiral Mayo, Commander in Chief of the U. S. Atlantic Fleet.

Salty, seasoned Admiral Ernest Joseph King was born November 23, 1878, in Lorain, Ohio, on the shores of freshwater Lake Erie. His father was employed by the Baltimore and Ohio Railroad as a master mechanic.

In the midst of his high school studies, he decided to go to work in a Cleveland metal pipe factory. He found that he didn't like the job any too well. However, his father insisted upon his finishing a full year at work before resuming his studies. Shortly after graduating from Lorain High, a competitive examination gave King his Annapolis appointment.

The Academy yearbook for the Class of 1901 calls Midshipman King "Court Beauty No. 2, with a laugh as rosy as his cheeks," and, "Temper—don't fool with nitroglycerine." Classmates remember calling apple-cheeked King Dolly.

The Spanish-American War interrupted young King's studies. Aboard ship in active service he was under fire during the blockade of Havana. After the war he went back to his studies to graduate fourth in a class of 67 students.

Midshipman King became Ensign King on June 7, 1903, after the two years of duty at sea then required by law. The young officer and Martha Egerton of Baltimore were married in 1905. In what was reputedly a race with a fellow officer, King produced six daughters before the lucky seventh turned out to be a boy, promptly named Ernest Joseph King, Jr. An English friend remarked," . . . should have been named Ernest Endeavor."

After several years of routine duties on surface ships, King, with the rank of captain, reported for submarine duty in July 1922. Fourteen months later

he took command of the base at New London and distinguished himself by his masterly handling of salvage work on the sunken submarine *S-51*.

At the age of 48, King took time off from his command, a seaplane tender, to attend the Naval Air Station at Pensacola, Florida. He is one of the few senior naval officers to hold a pilot's license. Late that year, King was once more directing salvage operations, this time the unfortunate *S-4*, on the bottom off Provincetown.

August 1928 found King serving as Assistant Chief of the Bureau of Aeronautics, then commander of the Naval Air Station at Norfolk, Virginia. His next command was as captain of the famous carrier, *Lexington*. After a course in the Naval War College, King became Chief of the Bureau of Aeronautics, replacing Admiral Moffett, lost when the dirigible *Akron* crashed at sea. Several more assignments ended with King's elevation to Rear Admiral.

With the Atlantic infested with Axis U-boats and war raging on two continents, King assumed command of the U. S. Fleet Patrol Force. In February, 1941, with the rank of admiral, he became Commander in Chief of the Atlantic Fleet. He took the post of Commander in Chief of the U. S. Fleet shortly after Japan's attack on Pearl Harbor.

In a series of moves to streamline the Naval High Command, the President combined the offices of Commander in Chief of the U. S. Fleet and Chief of Naval Operations, thus giving Admiral King the most complete authority ever held by any U. S. naval officer.

King has carefully prepared himself for the position he now holds, by thorough training in the three main branches of naval operations, air, surface, and submarine.

Today tall, lean Admiral Ernest Joseph King is master of the gigantic, sprawling U. S. Navy. Under the general direction of the Secretary of the Navy, he is responsible only to the President of the United States, his personal and intimate friend since Navy Department days of the last war.

On December 15, 1944, Admiral King was given the new 5-star rank, Admiral of the Fleet.

T.H. Chamberlain

ADMIRAL CHESTER WILLIAM NIMITZ

UNITED STATES NAVY

When Chester Nimitz was a towheaded, gangling boy in Fredericksburg, Texas, his white-bearded old grandfather used to take him up to the upper deck of the town's first hotel and tell the lad stories of life at sea. The old sea captain, Charles H. Nimitz, had settled in the little Germanic village after an adventurous life afloat. He built a hotel that had a top deck like a steamer and a bridge above that. The hotel could be seen for miles.

Chester's father died before he was born, February 24, 1885, and the grandfather devoted the rest of his life to raising the boy.

The family moved to Kerrville, Texas, where young Nimitz attended high school. He entered the Naval Academy only after it was discovered that there were no vacancies in West Point, his first choice. The Navy almost lost a future admiral when Nimitz became very seasick while on an excursion trip across the bay, near Annapolis. At the Academy he was stroke on the crew although he was lighter than most of the men. He weighed only 150 pounds at the time.

Nimitz graduated with distinction in the class of 1905, seventh in his class, and after the required two years at sea, was commissioned an ensign on January 31, 1907. Not long after his graduation, Nimitz was in command of a leaky old torpedo boat, when the engine room began to fill. "She's going to sink!" came the engineer's voice up the speaking tube. "Look on page 84 of Barton's Engineering Manual. It tells you what to do . . ." calmly and typically replied young Nimitz. The old tub didn't sink.

Nimitz was in the Far East when he was detailed to the Asiatic Station in command of the USS *Panay*, predecessor of the gunboat of the same name "accidentally" sunk in the Yangtze River by Japanese bombers in 1937. The young ensign came back to the States in 1908 aboard the USS *Ranger*. Early in 1909, he reported to the First Submarine Flotilla for instruction. He was given command of the flotilla in May 1909, and was commissioned lieutenant, both grades, in January 1910.

One day in March 1912, Nimitz, in command of the Third Submarine Division, rescued a sailor from drowning.

About this time, Chester Nimitz and Catherine Freeman of Wollaston, Massachusetts, were married. The couple have three daughters and one son, Lt. Comdr. Chester W. Nimitz, Jr.

During the last war, Nimitz was on submarine duty as aide and later Chief of Staff to Admiral Robison, Commander, Submarine Force, Atlantic Fleet. In September 1918, Nimitz, a commander by that time, reported in Washington to the Office of the Chief of Naval Operations. He was later assigned additional duty as Senior Member, Board of Submarine Design, Navy Department. He became executive officer of the USS *South Carolina*, and then took command of the USS *Chicago* in June 1920, with additional duty as commander of Submarine Division Fourteen, based at Pearl Harbor. Two years later he was detached and went through a course of instruction at the Naval War College in Newport, Rhode Island.

In 1926, Nimitz installed, at the University of California, one of the first Naval Reserve Training Corps units. After serving as Assistant Chief of the Bureau of Navigation for three years he attained flag rank in June 1938, and command of Battleship Division One, Battle Force.

On December 17, 1941, ten days after the Japanese assault on Pearl Harbor, Nimitz was detached from his position as Chief of the Bureau of Navigation and ordered to duty as Commander in Chief of the Pacific Fleet, with the rank of admiral. He assumed that command on December 31.

A citation presented to Admiral Nimitz, along with the Distinguished Service Medal, reads: "For exceptionally meritorious service as Commander in Chief . . . His conduct of the operations of the Pacific Fleet, resulting in successful actions against the enemy in the Coral Sea, May 1942, and off Midway Island in June 1942, was characterized by unfailing judgment and sound decision, coupled with skill and vigor. His exercise of command on all occasions left nothing to be desired."

His classmates at Annapolis, long before, had said in the yearbook, "He possesses that calm and steadygoing Dutch way that gets at the bottom of things . . . delights in a rough house . . . a mixer of famous punches."

On December 15, 1944, Admiral Nimitz was given the new 5-star rank, Admiral of the Fleet.

ADMIRAL HAROLD RAYNSFORD STARK

UNITED STATES NAVY

"You can't buy yesterday with dollars," was the message hammered home to congressional leaders by Admiral Stark, who, as chief of Naval Operations, nursed his cherished two-ocean Navy into being. To this mild mannered, ruddy, silver-haired naval strategist must go the major credit for the Navy's rapid growth from 1939 until the United States' entry into the present war.

Stark was born November 12, 1880, in land-locked, coal mining Wilkes-Barre, Pennsylvania, the son of Benjamin Franklin Stark. As a boy he sailed small boats on near-by Lake Carey, one of the factors which influenced his choice of a Navy career. He obtained an appointment to Annapolis and in 1899 after four years of study and the required two years afloat he received his commission.

Young Naval Academy plebe Stark was tagged Betty by upperclassmen who, as a hazing stunt, made him stop, place his hand over his heart and exclaim, "We'll win today, or Betty Stark's a widow," a saying attributed to Revolutionary War Gen. John Stark. Most history books however, refer to the lady in question as Molly. The Naval Academy yearbook, *The Log*, described young Stark as, "musical—having made the day hideous with singing."

After Ensign Stark's marriage in 1907 to his childhood playmate and sailing companion, Katherine Adele Rhoades, he was assigned a series of destroyer commands and by 1917 was head of the Asiatic Fleet Flotilla. He was awarded the Distinguished Service Medal with this citation: "For exceptionally meritorious service during the World War, in a duty of great responsibility as a commander of a squadron of small and old destroyers hurriedly fitted out in the Philippines and dispatched to the Mediterranean at a season when the southwest monsoon was at its height." The squadron arrived in record time and took an active part in the anti-submarine campaign.

Detailed to London, Stark became Recruiting Officer and aide to Admiral Sims, Commander of U. S. Naval Forces in European waters.

Following a series of duty tours as executive officer and naval inspector in various stations, Commander Stark became a captain in June 1926 Over a

three-year period he was Naval Aide to two Secretaries of the Navy. A year at sea followed and then Stark became head of the Navy's Ordnance Bureau where under his watchful eye the Navy's unique, secret, remote fire control system was perfected.

Admiral Stark returned to sea duty in the Pacific and while in command of Cruisers, Battle Force, he was chosen to succeed Admiral Leahy as Chief of Naval Operations in August, 1939.

Of medium height, soft voiced, bespectacled Admiral Stark is rated a sound thinker, calm and level-headed in his decisions. He is an excellent administrator, noted for the clarity and conciseness of his official orders.

In peacetime the admiral found time for an occasional golf game and enjoyed small boat sailing. His real hobby is the taking of excellent color movies of scenes in ports around the world. While at sea his aides were instructed to awaken him before dawn so that exceptionally brilliant sunrises could be preserved on film for home projection.

Back in 1914 the then Assistant Secretary of the Navy was aboard a destroyer commanded by young Lieutenant Stark. The Secretary, in familiar waters off Campobello Island, asked to be allowed to take the helm. Stark refused. Twenty-five years later the former Assistant Secretary, now President Franklin D. Roosevelt, chose Stark for the important role of Chief of Naval Operations.

Given full credit for his success in building and training the United States two-ocean Navy in a presidential citation, Stark was sent to London in 1942 to coordinate British-American anti-submarine measures and to head U. S. Naval Forces in European waters during the amphibious assault on the Axis-dominated continent of Europe.

" . . . Through keen foresight and exceptional administrative ability, Admiral Stark was able to plan for and meet the necessary personnel and material requirements for this enormous operation. Only through his untiring efforts was the accomplishment of this successful invasion completed." So reads an Army citation presented to Admiral Harold Raynsford Stark together with the Army's Distinguished Service Medal.

★ ★ 38 ★ ★

ADMIRAL WILLIAM FREDERICK HALSEY, JR.

UNITED STATES NAVY

"Don't let that happen," Admiral Halsey boomed at reporters after relating his great worry, that the Pacific War might end before he had a chance to pound the Japanese mainland. This conversation took place in Washington just before Halsey assumed his Third Fleet Command.

William Frederick Halsey, Jr., has spent his lifetime in the Navy. He was born in Elizabeth, New Jersey, October 30, 1882, the son of a naval officer then stationed in the Pacific. His mother recalls that the father, home after three years, immediately took his small son to the barber to shear off his long golden curls.

Asked what schools he had attended before his enrollment at Annapolis, Bull Halsey replied, "Many—and the University of Virginia." Actually he had a typical Navy education, going to school in Elizabeth, Coronado, San Francisco, and Annapolis.

President McKinley appointed him to the Naval Academy in 1900. Halsey was in the University of Virginia studying medicine and, as he relates it, would have been a doctor today if his mother hadn't dogged the President until he gave her the appointment to get rid of her.

Halsey proved to be an indifferent student but an aggressive football player, winning the Thompson cup for athletics. Sportswriters, nicknaming him Bull, called Halsey a good player on a poor team. The Academy Yearbook referred to him as "A real old salt . . . looks like a figurehead of Neptune." He was graduated forty-third in his class of 62.

The future Admiral began his seagoing career on board the old battleship *Missouri* in 1904. He has since logged up 25 years afloat, a record exceeded only by King and Nimitz, his present superiors.

Ensign Halsey made the famous 1908 cruise around the world as an officer of the USS *Kansas* with the Battle Fleet.

Halsey met and married Frances Cooke Grandy of Norfolk, Virginia, at about this time. He had overcome her southern family's objections to having a Yankee Navy officer as a son-in-law.

By the time of the last war Halsey was a lieutenant commander and had served in a number of varied commands. He was known as a man of action, daring and impetuous, a specialist in destroyer maneuvers. At the outbreak of war in 1917 he was an executive officer at the Naval Academy. Halsey was transferred to Queenstown, Ireland, for duty with the destroyer force there.

In 1921 he was detailed to Naval Intelligence, a shore duty, and then for two years he was naval attaché in Berlin with additional duties in Copenhagen and Stockholm.

His next ten years were spent in routine ship and shore stations. By 1934 Halsey had taken advanced courses at both the Naval and Army War Colleges and had applied for admission to the Pensacola Naval Air School. Broad faced, popular, zestful Bull breezed through the difficult base course without effort even though he was over 50 years old at the time. Since then he has logged up over 1,500 hours flying time.

Halsey was commander of the carrier *Saratoga* for two years and after a stretch as Commandant of the Pensacola Air Base, he was promoted to rear admiral in 1938 and took command of Carrier Division Two, stationed in the Pacific. In June 1940 with the rank of vice admiral, Halsey hoisted his three-star flag over his flagship, the carrier *Enterprise*.

On December 7, 1941, Admiral Halsey was at sea with his squadron on his way back to Pearl Harbor when the Japanese attack began. As senior officer afloat he was ordered to take command of all ships at sea in the area. During the trying period at the start of the war Halsey was at sea on patrol and on February 1, 1942, his carrier force, in an attack on the enemy bases in the Marshall Islands, gave the Japanese a foretaste of what was in store for them.

Halsey was in command of the carrier force that moved in close enough to Japan to launch Doolittle on his historic Tokyo raid. In October 1942 Admiral King gave him command of all U. S. Forces in the South Pacific.

The admiral is generally regarded by fellow officers and men as the Navy's greatest fighting man since Admiral Dewey. Outwardly calm, his face flushes with excitement at the approach of action. His signal flags give him away as they are hoisted. They spell out, "Get closer."

T. H. Chamberlain

ADMIRAL ROYAL EASON INGERSOLL

UNITED STATES NAVY

During the World War Ingersoll brilliantly organized and headed the Office of Naval Communications in Washington. He was ordered to report to Paris and sailed within three days, on the tenth of November. The armistice was signed 24 hours later. "I was afloat for one day, anyway," he says.

At the Paris peace conference Ingersoll was placed in charge of the highly secret Naval Communications Office handling President Wilson's messages to and from Washington. When the President returned home on the *George Washington*, Ingersoll went along in the same capacity.

Royal Eason Ingersoll was born in Washington, D. C., June 20, 1883, the son of Rear Admiral Royal Rodney Ingersoll who had graduated from the Naval Academy in 1868. The younger Ingersoll attended public schools in La Porte, Indiana, and in 1901 he was appointed to Annapolis.

He was graduated with distinction in 1905 and spent two years at sea before he gained his coveted ensign's commission in February 1907.

Ensign Ingersoll was detailed to the Bureau of Ordnance when his previous ship, the USS *Connecticut*, started out on the 1908 World cruise as fleet flagship. Young Ingersoll caught up with the fleet in San Francisco and finished the rest of the trip aboard.

After attending the Naval War College in Newport, he taught seamanship and English at Annapolis for the next two years. By the beginning of the World War, Ingersoll was on active sea duty with the Asiatic Fleet and stationed in Shanghai. On his return to the United States he was ordered to duty in the Office of Communications.

Ingersoll's job in perfecting the Navy's communications system is still looked upon as a brilliant piece of work and fellow officers give him a major share of the credit for the development of the "unbreakable code" which Navy guards so zealously.

Early in his career the young officer married Louise Van Harlingen. Their son, Royal Rodney Ingersoll II, was graduated from the Naval Academy and killed aboard the carrier *Hornet* when a wounded pilot accidently tripped his machine-gun release while attempting to land.

At the outbreak of the present war in the Pacific,

Rear Admiral Ingersoll was serving as Assistant to the Chief of Naval Operations in Washington. He was little known outside naval circles but his superiors considered pipe-smoking, shy 'Budge' Ingersoll one of their best officers.

In the reshuffling of top naval commands that followed the war's beginning he was chosen to replace Admiral King as head of the Atlantic Fleet when the latter was made Naval Commander in Chief.

On New Year's Day, 1942, Ingersoll, now a vice admiral, took over his new duties. In six months he was promoted to full admiral, the U-boat menace was being checked and U. S. Forces were training in Britain for later invasions of the African and European continents. His was the overall responsibility for the successful transportation and protection of troops and matériel for both the African and Sicilian campaigns. He accomplished this last maneuver without the loss of a ship or a man.

In November 1944, the Navy Department shifted this quiet logistics expert from the Atlantic to the area most in need of his talents at the time. Given the status of Deputy Commander in Chief of the U. S. Fleet and Deputy Chief of Naval Operations, his assignment was to command the Western Sea Frontier and to accelerate and expand the flow of supplies across the Pacific in readiness for the coming all-out attack on Japan.

Four stars on his uniform haven't changed Budge Ingersoll's manner. He is just as unassuming as ever, likes to read, and work on his stamp collection, a hobby he has pursued since his boyhood. Ingersoll leads a calm, simple private life, "...as simple as any farmer's ever was..." remarked one of his fellow admirals. Secretary of the Navy Forrestal says that trying to get Admiral Ingersoll to talk is almost an impossibility and that he is the most silent man he's ever met. The admiral even has magazines sent to him as "Mr. R. E. Ingersoll."

Boston travellers were somewhat astonished a short while ago to see a four star admiral lugging some heavy suitcases through the crowds awaiting trains. It was Ingersoll, impatient at finding no porter available to carry a friend's luggage, taking matters into his own hands.

T.H. Chamberlain

ADMIRAL RAYMOND AMES SPRUANCE

UNITED STATES NAVY

Relatives of Admiral Spruance tell of the time in his early childhood when the family cook, after rescuing him from a well into which he had tumbled, said, "Look, I've saved an admiral."

Raymond Ames Spruance was born July 3, 1886, in Baltimore, Maryland, where his mother had gone to await his birth at her parents' home. He has always claimed Indiana as his home state and it was from there that he secured his appointment to Annapolis. While at the Naval Academy he was a quiet lad, nicknamed Sprew by his classmates. Even at that early date he made it a point to avoid undue publicity.

After his graduation he was detailed to several duty tours at sea and in 1916 he assisted in fitting out the new battleship *Pennsylvania* and served aboard her after she was commissioned.

Early in his career Spruance became a marked man for his knowledge of fire control methods. He went to London and Edinburgh for the Navy in connection with this work and in 1922 he was made a member of the board on doctrine of aircraft in connection with fleet fire control. He spent most of the last war attached to the Brooklyn Navy Yard, managing to spend about two months aboard a transport as its executive officer.

Spruance married Margaret Vance Dean of Indianapolis. They have two children, a son who was graduated from Annapolis in 1937, and a daughter.

By 1929 he had completed a Naval War College course and two years in the office of Naval Intelligence. By 1931, after a tour of sea duty, he was assigned to the Naval War College as a member of the staff. Shore and sea duties kept him busy until February 1940, when he was made Commandant of the Tenth Naval District, Headquarters, San Juan, Puerto Rico. In June 1942 Spruance was named Chief of Staff and aide to the Commander in Chief, Pacific Fleet. From that post he became Commander of the Central Pacific Force and later Commander, Fifth Fleet.

During the Midway battle a group of American patrol planes, almost out of gas after a long reconnaissance sweep, sighted a group of three enemy carriers and escorts. The flight leader asked permission to withdraw and refuel. "Attack at once," came the fateful order from Admiral Spruance on the bridge. Thus began the famous suicide run of Torpedo Eight Squadron, catching the Japanese off guard and turning back the enemy invasion fleet.

Naval attacks against enemy bases in the Gilbert and Marshall Islands and strikes against Japanese strongholds in Yap and the Palau Islands were carried out under Spruance's command. He was Commander, Central Pacific Fleet, during the occupation of the Gilbert Islands in November, 1943.

A citation given the Admiral at about this time reads, in part: "In command of Naval Forces and certain Army amphibious and air forces during the assaults on Tarawa, Makin and Apamama, Vice Admiral Spruance conducted this action with daring strategy and brilliant employment of the units of his command."

His superior officer, Admiral Nimitz, says of him, "Nothing you can say about Spruance would be praise enough." He is pointed out as the model admiral, good looking, compact, gimlet-eyed, intelligent and self disciplined. He was awarded the four stars of a full admiral in February 1944, after his spectacular series of raids in the Pacific area in enemy waters.

War and combat duties have not changed the Admiral's ingrained personal habits, his friends say. He likes to listen to good music while thinking out a problem. A non-drinker, he is a good mixer with an excellent sense of humor. A man of few words, Spruance speaks with a hoosier drawl.

Spruance is known as an indefatigable hiker even aboard ship. At the regulation 132 steps per minute, he covers eight or ten miles a day, shirtless in warm weather to absorb the sun's rays. Cracked a correspondent, "He will win the war in a walk—literally."

Fellow officers refer to Sprew as a "cold-blooded fighting fool," a man dedicated to a single objective, to win the war for his country.

Of his job he says, "The object of Navy tactics is to use all of the weapons that you have at your command."

T. H. Chamberlain

VICE ADMIRAL JOHN HENRY TOWERS

UNITED STATES NAVY

Square, stocky, greying, blue-eyed and stern, the Navy's No. 1 aviator, sole survivor of the first trio of naval men to become pilots, stood at his chest-high desk in the Navy Department making ready to take over his duties with the Fleet in the Pacific. Admiral Towers looks upon battleships and planes as equally indispensible in warfare. "A naval aviator is part of a team," he says. "If he doesn't practice with the team, he won't know the signals." Although he is an air power enthusiast, he is a firm advocate of the Navy's doctrine that the air forces remain a component part of the battle fleet.

John Henry Towers was born in Rome, Georgia, January 30, 1885. After his local schooling his application was turned down by the Annapolis authorities. Towers spent two years in Georgia Tech before he was finally admitted to the Naval Academy. He graduated in 1906 as a Passed Midshipman, and was assigned aboard the USS *Kentucky*. Later as an ensign Towers became spotter and fire control officer on the battleship *Michigan*. The *Michigan* won the Gunnery Trophy in 1911. Promoted to lieutenant, Towers applied for aviation training and was sent to Hammondsport, New York, for flight instruction under Glenn Curtiss.

Within three months Towers had qualified as an aviator, according to regulations then in force. He was shifted to Annapolis. From there he became test pilot for Curtiss in California, flying experimental seaplanes at North Island, San Diego.

In October 1912, Lieutenant Towers established a world's record with an endurance flight of six hours, ten minutes, using a Curtiss seaplane, while in charge of the Naval Aviation Camp at Annapolis.

One day in June 1912, while flying as a passenger in a Wright seaplane, both Towers and the pilot were thrown clear when the plane was caught in an atmospheric disturbance. The pilot dropped to his death 1,700 feet below. Towers managed to grasp a projection of the seaplane and fell with it, suffering severe injuries. As a result of this accident, safety belts were thereafter required on all naval planes.

Lieutenant Towers was sent to Guantanamo Bay, Cuba, to experiment with the fleet in operational work. During the Mexican border trouble Towers was Executive Officer of the Naval Aviation unit at the landings in Vera Cruz and Tampico. The unit consisted of four planes.

War in Europe in 1914 caused the abandonment of a projected trans-atlantic flight sponsored by Rodman Wanamaker, and Towers was ordered abroad as an aviation observer attached to the American Embassy in London. In 1916, he was brought back to Washington, detailed to the office of the Chief of Naval Operations, and after helping organize the Naval Flying Corps was appointed Assistant Director of Naval Aviation.

In 1919, now a commander, Towers helped organize and was second in command of the historic flight of the *NC* seaplanes in the Navy's first attempt to fly an air group across the Atlantic Ocean. All the squadron except the *NC-4* fell by the wayside, including Towers' own, the *NC-3*. Forced down within 300 miles of the Azores, in a rough sea, he taxied the remainder of the distance to safety.

For the next seven years he was assigned a variety of stations and served as Naval Attaché in several American embassies in Europe. By January 1927 he was commander of the *Langley*, first United States aircraft carrier. Transferred to the Bureau of Aeronautics as head of the planning division he was made Assistant Chief and promoted to captain in 1929. He also served as a member of the National Advisory Committee for Aeronautics at the invitation of President Hoover.

In 1937, Captain Towers was given command of the then largest vessel in the Navy, the aircraft carrier *Saratoga*. A year later, back at his old job in the Bureau of Aeronautics he was made Chief of the Bureau and a rear admiral in June 1939. In September 1942 he was ordered to duty as Air Force Commander, Pacific Fleet with the rank of vice admiral. Later he was made Deputy Commander in Chief, Pacific Fleet.

Considered handsome in his youth, Admiral Towers still deserves the description. Married twice, he has a son and a daughter by his first wife.

VICE ADMIRAL HENRY KENT HEWITT

UNITED STATES NAVY

Admiral Hewitt was the man entrusted with the overall command of one of the largest convoys in all history. His was the responsibility of bringing to the coast of French Morocco on a fixed date in November 1942 a motley collection of mine layers, battleships, troopships, ammunition and supply ships of all categories. If you visualize Hewitt nervously pacing his bridge as the convoy zig-zagged its way through mine and Axis submarine-infested waters you are mistaken. "I had quite a lot on my mind, but I slept well," Admiral Hewitt relates. "I ate too much and put on weight."

Hewitt says that the Army-Navy teamwork was so smooth that it was impossible for him to tell at just what point his authority ceased and that of fire-eating General Patton began.

The Admiral's dexterity in the handling of big-scale amphibious landings was called upon in the highly successful Sicily operation and again at the time of the landings in Southern France. The citation given him afterwards reads: ". . . Admiral Hewitt was responsible for all naval activities in connection with the invasion of Southern France. Displaying great technical skill, efficiency, and a broad knowledge of the tremendous task entrusted to him, he coordinated all naval activities of both United States and Allied Forces involved in the operation."

Henry Kent Hewitt was born in Hackensack, New Jersey, February 11, 1887. After attending the local high school, he secured an appointment to the Naval Academy in 1903. He was a member of the class of 1907 which was graduated a year early, in 1906. After his graduation he served aboard several different ships until, due to his excellent standing in mathematics, he was detailed to Annapolis as an instructor.

Ordered back to sea in mid-1916, Hewitt took command of the USS *Eagle*. In June of 1918, with the submarine blockade going full blast, Hewitt reported for duty with the Destroyer Force stationed at Brest, France. As commander of the destroyer *Cummings*, he was awarded the Navy Cross for his convoy and anti-sub work.

Hewitt became a teacher again when the war was over, being assigned once more to the Naval Academy. This time he was in the Department of Electrical Engineering and Physics. In 1921 he went to sea again as gunnery officer aboard the battleship *Pennsylvania*. This assignment lasted until 1923 when he was ordered to the Fleet Training Division in Washington for a three-year period.

In September, 1926, Hewitt took up his duties as aide to Admiral Louis R. de Steiguer aboard the battleship *West Virginia*. He was also Fleet Gunnery Officer and aide to the admiral when he commanded the Battle Fleet.

Sent through the Naval War College at Newport, Rhode Island, Hewitt remained there for two more years as an instructor before going to sea again as commander of Destroyer Division Twelve. After a year he was transferred to duty as Force Operations Officer on Staff of the Fleet Battle Force.

Once more teaching at the Naval Academy, Hewitt served a three-year hitch as head of the Department of Mathematics until March 1936 when he became commanding officer of the cruiser *Indianapolis* at the time President Roosevelt sailed to the Pan-American Peace Conference at Buenos Aires.

Detached from the *Indianapolis* in 1937, Hewitt became Chief of Staff and aide to the commander of the Cruiser Scouting Force, then for a time he became Chief Inspector of the naval ammunition depot on Puget Sound. His next duty was as commander of the Special Service Squadron in the Canal Zone.

By June 1941, Hewitt was in command of all Atlantic Fleet cruisers with added personal command of a cruiser division. In preparation for the African invasion Hewitt was made Commander of the Amphibious Force, Atlantic Fleet. For his efforts in the several invasion landings under his supervision he was given both the Army and Navy Distinguished Service Medals.

Friends of Admiral Hewitt assert that he is fond of taking extremely brisk walks ashore with the avowed purpose of removing some of the excess weight he puts on in the course of his strenuous duties at sea.

VICE ADMIRAL THOMAS CASSIN KINKAID

UNITED STATES NAVY

Old naval traditions hold that most officers and men in the service come from the Midwest. Supposedly they take to blue water because they don't know any better.

Thomas Cassin Kinkaid is one notable exception to this legend. As the son of Rear Admiral Thomas Wright Kinkaid he has spent his lifetime around naval ships and establishments. As a Navy junior his career was planned for him at an early age. He attended Western High School in Washington, D. C., and in 1904 was appointed to the Naval Academy by President Theodore Roosevelt.

At the Academy the class yearbook has this to say about "Kink" in 1908, "A black-eyed, rosy-cheeked, noisy Irishman, who loves a rough house and the training table grub . . . he has a corking good disposition and is in every way a man of the first order."

Admiral Kinkaid is still called "a man of the first order" by the men who have fought with him. He probably has been in more shooting scrapes with the Japanese than any other senior naval officer and is known to be absolutely fearless. One story relates that while under a particularly vicious enemy air attack Kinkaid, on the bridge of the carrier *Enterprise*, stood in a torn shirt, smoking a cigarette and issuing orders with aplomb while all the other officers dived headlong for cover.

After his Annapolis graduation, Kinkaid, as a specialist in ordnance, fell heir to a series of choice assignments. He served aboard the battleships *Pennsylvania* and *Arizona* during the last war and was gunnery officer on the *Arizona* in 1918.

A period of his official life that the admiral likes to recall is the two years spent as Assistant Chief of Staff to Rear Admiral Mark L. Bristol with a U. S. naval detachment in Turkish waters.

After commanding the USS *Isherwood* for two years plus a tour of duty at the Naval Gun Factory in Washington he became gunnery officer for the U. S. Fleet and aide to the Commander in Chief.

Later, after completing the senior course at the Naval War College, Kinkaid, then a commander, was given the post of Secretary of the important General Board. The experience gained in this job

helped to prepare him for his next assignment, naval advisor to the American members of the 1932 Disarmament Conference held at Geneva, Switzerland. Here Kinkaid was able to put to good use his social training. He is a good conversationalist, a reasonable drinker, and plays a decent game of bridge, tennis, and golf.

Back in the United States, he became executive officer aboard the battleship *Colorado*, again among his beloved big guns.

Late in 1938 Kinkaid was detailed to the American Embassy in Rome and from there to Belgrade. In March 1941 he was given a command at sea. He attained flag rank on November 17, 1941.

The Distinguished Service Medal was presented to Vice Admiral Kinkaid by Admiral Nimitz in 1942 for his skill and devotion to duty in the Battle of the Coral Sea. In January 1943, for his part in the Battle of the Solomon Islands, he won a Gold Star, equivalent to a second DSM. Shortly afterwards a third citation and another Gold Star were presented to Kinkaid in recognition of his work as Commander of the North Pacific Force. This is the fleet used in the difficult and dangerous operations that resulted in the withdrawal of the Japanese occupation forces in the Aleutians, on Attu and Kiska Islands.

In November 1943 he became Commander, Naval Forces, Southwest Pacific, comprising the Seventh Fleet. In the naval actions accompanying MacArthur's return to the Philippines he further distinguished himself. As Seventh Fleet Commander, Kinkaid was detailed to protect Army Ground Forces from imminent Japanese fleet attacks. Warned of the enemy's approach he calmly calculated his risks, split his forces, and in twin attacks caused such severe losses that the enemy was forced to limp back to their bases, without inflicting any damage to MacArthur's forces.

Thomas Cassin Kinkaid was born in Hanover, New Hampshire, April 3, 1888, and is married to the former Helen Ross of Philadelphia.

Among his friends Kinkaid is known as a good solid citizen, in no sense a "trick" admiral but a courageous man against any odds.

T.H. Chamberlain

VICE ADMIRAL RICHMOND KELLY TURNER

UNITED STATES NAVY

When the United States declared war in December 1941, R. Kelly Turner, as he signs his paychecks, was quietly working in the War Plans Division of the Navy Department in Washington. In the summer of 1942 Turner was in charge of Navy operations at Guadalcanal. He says that he became intrigued with the possibilities of amphibious operations and wangled himself the job as commander of the South Pacific Amphibious Force involved in the landings.

The historic struggle at Guadalcanal and Tulagi is well known but few people realize that Turner was forced to launch the drive with only partly completed preparations. He says, "It was a question of doing it immediately or not at all." Three days after he arrived in New Zealand by plane he was on his way to Guadalcanal with a staff he'd never seen before and a fleet that had never maneuvered together. Turner afterward led operations that put troops ashore at New Georgia, Tarawa, and Makin Islands.

Richmond Kelly Turner was born in Portland, Oregon, May 27, 1885. He attended high school in Stockton, California, and was appointed to the Naval Academy in 1904. At Annapolis he was a member of the track team, manager of the baseball team, and editor-in-chief of the school annual, *The Lucky Bag*, for 1908, the year of his graduation. Turner stood fifth in a class of 196. He finished two years at sea, then required by law, before he was commissioned ensign June 6, 1910.

In 1913 the Navy ordered Turner to Annapolis for postgraduate study in ordnance engineering, later to Bethlehem Steel Co., Columbia University, and the Indian Head proving ground in Maryland. After completing this course he was made lieutenant in 1916 and detailed to the battleship *Michigan*. During most of the last war Turner filled the post of gunnery officer aboard various ships.

In July 1919 he went to the Navy Yard in Washington for a three-year stretch. Several years at sea followed and in the spring of 1924 Turner was in the Bureau of Ordnance in Washington.

At the age of 41 Kelly Turner reported to the Pensacola Air Station for flight training and was designated a Naval Aviator on August 30, 1927.

He then assumed command of the USS *Jason* and the duty of Commander, Aircraft Squadrons, Asiatic Fleet. He returned to Washington to serve in the Bureau of Aeronautics from 1929 through 1932 when he was sent to the Disarmament Conference at Geneva, Switzerland.

Turner next was detailed to the carrier *Saratoga* and later became Chief of Staff to the Commander, Aircraft, Battle Force of which the *Saratoga* was the flagship. In 1935 Captain Turner went through the senior course at the Naval War College, then served on the staff two years.

In October 1940 Turner reported as Director, War Plans Division, Office of the Chief of Naval Operations. Three months before Pearl Harbor he was made a rear admiral and shortly afterward was given additional duty as Assistant Chief of Staff to the Commander in Chief, U. S. Fleet. It was on July 18, 1942, that Rear Admiral Turner assumed command of the Amphibious Force that was to make history at Guadalcanal.

Admiral Turner is as forceful and stern a disciplinarian as any officer in the Navy. He is an untiring worker and expects the same quality in his men. He does not like yes-men and will listen to a junior officer who disagrees with his views. He's a man who will take a risk if the probable gain is great enough. He is a complete believer in co-ordination of the services.

He is known as Kelly to his contemporaries and to a few long-time intimates as Spuds. He explains that he has the longest Irish upper lip in the Navy. He likes to tend his flower garden when at home. He is tall and walks with a stately tread. Turner has bushy eyebrows above hard, grey eyes which peer out from behind glasses. He is partly bald with a fringe of grey hair.

The youngest of seven children, Turner's boyhood ambition was to be a lawyer until friends suggested that he try for Annapolis. His father was a newspaperman and, unlike most of the conservative, press-fearing Navy hierarchy, Kelly Turner believes that Americans should be told everything, both good and bad, as soon as possible. He says, "It's their war and they can take it. They've got to."

VICE ADMIRAL MARC ANDREW MITSCHER

UNITED STATES NAVY

A shy, mild appearing, wizened little man who resembles a veteran baseball umpire although he speaks in a near-whisper led carrier strikes against Truk, Saipan, Palau; commanded aircraft in the Solomons, and skippered the *Hornet* when that carrier played Shangri-La to Jimmy Doolittle's bombers for their famed Tokyo raid in 1942.

He's Vice Admiral Marc Andrew Mitscher, one of the Navy's earliest airmen and one of Japan's most feared enemies. Born in Wisconsin, he attended public schools in Washington, D. C., before his appointment to Annapolis in 1906. While at the Naval Academy he was dismissed for hazing but was allowed to resign. Then he was reinstated. His average grade for the four-year course was 2.5, the passing grade.

In 1915, five years after his graduation from Annapolis, he reported to Pensacola, Florida, where he won his Navy wings and became No. 32 on the list of naval aviators. Then he began making history in naval aviation.

He participated in early catapult experiments, commanded naval air stations on Long Island and in Miami, Florida, and in 1919 piloted the *NC-1* on the first Navy trans-Atlantic flight. For this feat he was awarded the Navy Cross, first of seven American medals he holds. The next year, from the USS *Aroostook*, he commanded the detachment of Air Forces at the fleet base in San Diego, California.

He served with the Bureau of Aeronautics in Washington and in 1937 became commanding officer of the USS *Wright*. Two years later he returned to the Bureau as Assistant Chief.

Mitscher commissioned the *Hornet* in 1941 and served as her commanding officer until June 1942. During that period she participated in the Battle of Midway and was known to the Japs as the "Blue Ghost of the Pacific." He assumed command of Patrol Wing Two in April 1943; then was given a tough job, Commander Air, Solomon Islands. The wiry little man with the bushy eyebrows used a field trunk as an office and performed the double job of keeping up steady air attacks on the enemy and building new bomber bases.

He made quick, accurate decisions in sending up the proper number of fighters to knock Jap planes from the air and cannily figured when the enemy was about to strike in time to knock out quantities of Jap planes on the ground. He won the Distinguished Service Medal for this service.

When he left the Solomons his chief desire was "to get an aircraft carrier and get loose in the Central Pacific." He got his wish and as commander of a carrier task force he attacked the Marshalls, Truk, and Saipan. He was awarded the Gold Star in lieu of a second Distinguished Service Cross with a citation which reads, in part: "As a result of Vice Admiral Mitscher's brilliant leadership and indomitable fighting spirit, the Central Pacific Force obtained and maintained complete control of the air throughout this vital area."

Wearing his famous long-visored khaki cap, he presents a strange figure as he sits in his swivel chair on the flat bridge riding backward. Dryly, he explains, "After 40 years of looking ahead, I've reached the age where I can start looking backwards. Actually it is to keep the wind out of my face." That rawboned face, extremely weathered and reddened, shows he hasn't kept out of many winds.

Mitscher was born in Hillsboro, Wisconsin, January 26, 1887, but was appointed to the Academy from Oklahoma. At Annapolis he was nicknamed Oklahoma Pete which was later shortened to Pete. Oklahoma is now home to him, and Mrs. Mitscher is waiting for him in Oklahoma City.

The man who says of the Japs, "You can't trust any of the devils. The only way to win is to kill so many they won't be able to exist as a nation," likes to fish and hunt but under no circumstance will he shoot a deer—"Their eyes," he explains.

His appointment to vice admiral was confirmed by the Senate May 25, 1944, to rank from the preceding March. The following August he was awarded a second Gold Star by Admiral Nimitz.

Mitscher's extreme hatred for the Japs is not the only reason behind his zeal in rooting them out of the Pacific. He received a brief, sincere letter of admiration from a 13-year-old boy. After reading it he looked up to remark in that quiet voice of his, "This is the sort of thing that makes a war worth fighting."

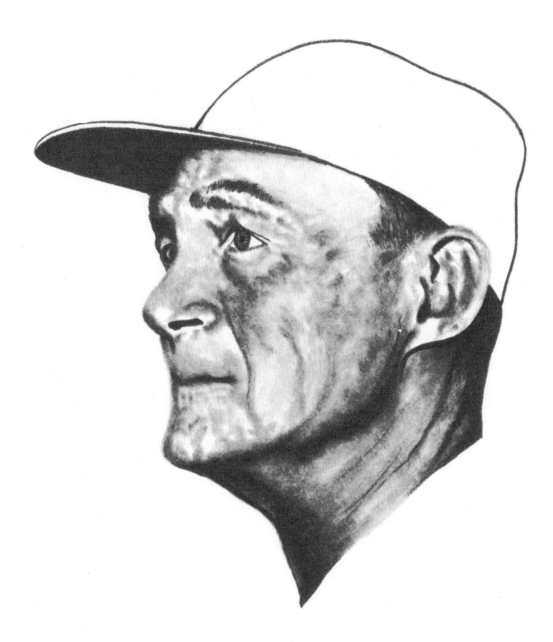

T.H. Chamberlain

VICE ADMIRAL CHARLES ANDREWS LOCKWOOD, JR.

UNITED STATES NAVY

Admiral Lockwood is commander of the Pacific Fleet Submarine Force, familiarly known as the "silent service." During wartime about all that can be said of the work being done by this branch of the Navy is, "Sh-h-h."

Quiet and a good listener, the admiral speaks softly and has an easy smile. High naval officials call him one of their best diplomats. Lockwood says that he is strictly a submarine man.

Charles Andrews Lockwood was born May 6, 1890, at Midland, Fauquier County, Virginia. He attended high school at Lamar, Missouri, and then Werntz's Preparatory School in Annapolis, prior to his appointment to the U. S. Naval Academy from Missouri in 1908. At the Academy he was an outstanding track athlete, setting the midshipman's one-mile record that stood for nearly 10 years. He was commissioned an ensign in June, 1912.

For two years following his graduation he served on two surface ships and for a time at the Naval Training Station, Great Lakes, Illinois. In June 1914 young Lockwood received orders to report to the Asiatic Station for instruction in submarines. During the last war, he was in command of three submarines at various times and later he was in command of the First Submarine Division, Asiatic Fleet.

Lockwood was detached from his command and ordered to Tokyo, Japan, to inspect ships purchased by the Navy and when that duty was completed in September 1918, he returned to the United States. Given command of the USS *G-1* and later the *N-5*, he was sent to join the American Naval Forces in European waters in February 1919. While in Europe he assumed command of the ex-German submarine, *UC-97*.

After Lockwood returned to the United States he fitted out and commanded under-sea craft until the spring of 1922 at which time he was sent once again to the Asiatic Station where he took command of the USS *Quiros* in June 1922 at Shanghai, China. Less than a year later he became aide and Flag Lieutenant on the staff of Rear Admiral W. W. Phelps, Commander of the Yangtze River Patrol.

In 1924 Lockwood reported at the Portsmouth Navy Yard for duty as repair officer. He was detached in May 1925 and ordered to fit out the new USS *V-3* and commanded her when she was commissioned. He went to Brazil as aide to the Chief of the Naval Mission for a year beginning in January 1929.

Lockwood was instructor at the Naval Academy from 1933 to 1935 and assumed command of Submarine Division 13 in September 1935. Then he spent two years with the Office of Chief of Naval Operations in Washington.

When Pearl Harbor was attacked Lockwood was Naval Attaché at the American Embassy in London. In May of 1942 he was ordered to command at sea followed by his promotion to rear admiral. When Rear Admiral English was killed in a plane crash, Lockwood became Commander of the Pacific Fleet Submarine Force and was promoted to the rank of vice admiral.

Vice Admiral Lockwood is known as a good listener. He says that there are two reasons for American success in sub warfare—the quality, training, and initiative of the commanders, and the subs themselves. "We've got the best damned submarines in the world," he says.

Young officers in the "silent service" regard Lockwood as one of their warmest personal friends. He knows them all by their first names and can recite their records in detail when he wants to prove a point.

Lockwood was married to Phyllis Irwin, daughter of Rear Admiral N. E. Irwin, in Brazil in January 1930. Admiral Irwin was in command of an American Naval Mission to Brazil. They have two sons and a daughter.

A masterpiece of understatement is this citation given to Admiral Lockwood: ". . . with great energy and persistence, he personally supervised careful investigation and planned tests to try out new ideas submitted by others. The results of these tests were most gratifying. Since that time, the increased efficiency has resulted in increased tonnage of enemy ships sunk and damaged . . ." What the citation really means will have to wait for publication until the end of the war when the stories of adventures of American under-sea craft in the broad reaches of the Pacific can be told. Until then stories about the "silent service" are strictly taboo.

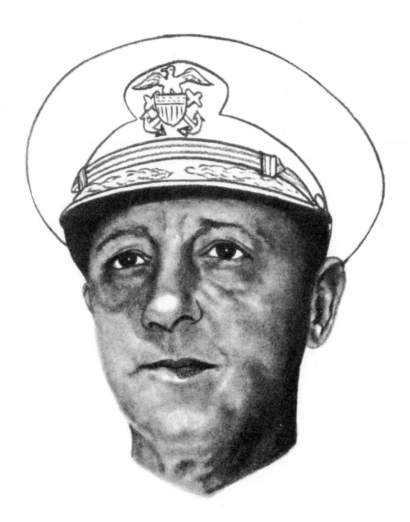

LIEUTENANT GENERAL ALEXANDER ARCHER VANDEGRIFT

UNITED STATES MARINE CORPS

General Vandegrift, with his never-failing smile and calm good humor has been given the nickname of Sunny Jim by his fellow Marines. During the struggle for the beaches and jungles of Guadalcanal, tired and emotionally exhausted officers from the battle area hurried into command headquarters to see Vandegrift. A short time later they would come out smiling and relaxed at some farewell sally from Sunny Jim. Even during the period of the most severe counterattacks by the Japanese, the General remained trim and confident. He managed to shave every day. Officers and correspondents could find Vandegrift sitting on a bench placed outside headquarters, always available for questions or a helping hand. He says that too much credit shouldn't be given him for keeping cool. "I'm just built that way," he says.

Vandegrift is fairly tall, with greying blond hair, rather thin on top. He has a very determined jaw, set in a ruddy, jovial face, and deep blue eyes with sun-wrinkles in the corners. He carries himself well and moves rapidly and nervously. He is fond of a good meal and relishes a touch of bourbon. Time has not changed his southern accent.

Alexander Archer Vandegrift was born in Charlottesville, Virginia, on March 13, 1887. He attended the University of Virginia for two years and still lists Charlottesville as his home. An appointment to West Point was his goal; however, the quota allowed his district was exhausted, so he applied to the Marines instead. He was commissioned a second lieutenant in the Marine Corps in January 1909.

Vandegrift's paternal grandfather had been a captain in the Confederate army and filled the young lad with stories of military life. This had quite a bearing on his choice of a career.

The General's life in the Marines has been packed with action. He has served in Cuba, Nicaragua, Mexico, Haiti, China and the South Pacific.

In 1912 he took part in the bombardment and capture of Coyotepe, Nicaragua. He participated in the occupation of Vera Cruz, Mexico, in 1914. A year later he was in Haiti, fighting against the hostile Cocos. His next few years were spent mostly with the Gendarmerie d'Haiti.

Vandegrift was brought back to the United States in 1923 and attended Marine Corps schools and was assigned duty tours inside the country until 1927, when he became Force Operations and Training Officer for the Marines at Shanghai, China, under the command of General Smedley Butler. Vandegrift also saw service in Pekin and Tientsin during this period. While stationed in the Orient he had several brushes with the wily Japanese and conceived his present dislike and distrust for them. Vandegrift's first real contact with them came when he ordered Marine Corps planes to rout some Jap observation planes hovering too close to U. S. Asiatic Fleet maneuvers.

From 1929 to 1933, Vandegrift was Assistant to the Chief Coordinator of the Budget Bureau. After that he became Assistant Chief of Staff, Fleet Marine Force. Next he was Executive Officer and finally Commandant of the detachment of Marines stationed at the American Embassy in Peiping, China, during the critical days from 1935 to the spring of 1937.

Brought back to Washington, Vandegrift became Secretary of the Marine Corps Commandant, then, raised to the rank of brigadier general, he was assigned as Assistant Commandant. He was sworn in as Commandant of the greatly expanded Corps, January 1, 1944, replacing General Thomas Holcomb, retired. To fill this position, the highest in the Marine Corps, General Vandegrift was called back from the South Pacific after successfully leading the first U. S. land offensive against the Japanese in the present war.

In action Vandegrift is not a dashing, spectacular fighter. He insists that he is "just a man doing his job," and seeing to it that others do theirs. During the fighting on Guadalcanal one of Vandegrift's colonels sent back word that he was withdrawing his men under heavy enemy fire, instead of advancing as ordered. Orders promptly went out for the second in command to take over. The regiment advanced and the colonel was shipped back home. When superiors asked if his Marines could hold the beachhead during the first Jap suicide attacks on Guadalcanal, General Vandegrift replied," Hell yes, why not?"

T.H. Chamberlain

LIEUTENANT GENERAL HOLLAND McTYEIRE SMITH

UNITED STATES MARINE CORPS

"What *are* the Marines?" Holland Smith asked his congressman back in 1905. Smith had come to Washington after graduating from the University of Alabama with a law degree, intending to obtain a commission in the Army. The secretary, in explaining that there were no vacancies, suggested that his friend try the Marines. Smith did so . . . and became a lieutenant general.

In the South Pacific battle areas "Howlin' Mad" Smith presents an incongruous figure in his rough, sloppy jungle dress, hopping about the beachhead shouting profane remarks at the Japs. His blue eyes peer brightly through steel rimmed glasses. His doughty face is topped off with a thatch of thinning, sandy hair. Fellow Marines have been calling him Howlin' Mad since his early days in the Philippines. Smith is also known as a front-line Charley for his eagerness to get up where shells are popping.

During preliminary bombardments, when General Smith is aboard the command ship, he is constantly in and out of the staff room, either peering at maps or at the shore. He chews on a cigar and sends a stream of appropriate epithets along with the beachhead-bound assault troops. As soon as a landing spot has been secured, Howlin' Mad Smith hops into a landing barge with his carbine under his arm and heads shoreward. He is rough, tough, noisy, but thoroughly human. Once as he was inspecting an area that had supposedly been mopped up, some concealed Japs let go a burst of mortar fire. Smith dived headlong for a foxhole, sat in it for a moment, then sheepishly said, "Hell, looks kind of silly for a general." When the next burst came Smith stood upright with the others. He becomes very moody and depressed when casualties have been heavy. As the men were going down the landing nets into assault boats during one of the landings a correspondent remarked on how young and fit they looked.

"Too bad most of them will be dead this time next year," Smith said as he gazed through misty glasses.

When a plan or order is being discussed Smith is a very reasonable man but, once settled, instructions must be carried out to the letter or Smith lives up to his nickname, Howlin' Mad.

Holland McTyeire Smith was born in Seale, Russel County, Alabama, April 20, 1882. He was graduated from Alabama Polytechnic Institute in 1901 with a bachelor of science degree. In 1903 he received a degree in law from the University of Alabama. Smith was appointed a second lieutenant of Marines in March 1905.

Lieutenant Smith spent the next few years on duty tours, mostly in the Philippines. He was on expeditionary duty in Panama in 1909.

During the last war Smith was in France with the Fourth Marine Brigade as adjutant in the Verdun sector. He participated in the Aisne-Marne Offensive as Assistant Operations Officer of the First Corps, First Army; in September and October 1918 Smith was in the St. Mihiel and Meuse-Argonne Offensives. The French awarded him the Croix de Guerre with palm.

Smith was Chief of Staff of the First Brigade, Marines, in Haiti from March 1924 to August 1925. He was Force Marine Officer, and aide on the Staff of the Commander, Battle Force, U. S. Fleet, from June 1933 to January 1935. He commanded the Marine Barracks in Washington, was Director of Division of Operations and Training, and Assistant to the Commandant successively until September 1939, at which time he assumed command of the First Marine Brigade of the Fleet Marine Force.

In 1941 the Amphibious Force, Atlantic Fleet, was organized with the First Marine Division and other Marine, Army, and Navy units as component parts and with Maj. Gen. Holland Smith as Commanding General. In October 1942 he became Commanding General of the Headquarters Company, Amphibious Corps, Pacific Fleet. As Commander of the Fleet Marine Force in the Pacific he has seen his gallant Leathernecks take islands from Guadalcanal to Guam. Smith is known as the most outstanding proponent of amphibious operations. He worked with Andrew Jackson Higgins in 1939 to help create a fast, shallow-draft landing boat and with Donald Roebling on his amphibious tractor. The tanks and landing craft used in Europe and the Pacific reflect these experiments. Smith has been called "the father of modern amphibious warfare."

T. H. Chamberlain.

VICE ADMIRAL RUSSELL RANDOLPH WAESCHE

UNITED STATES COAST GUARD

Long before the Japanese wheeled down out of the sky over Pearl Harbor on December 7, 1941, thousands of motorboats, manned by civilians enrolled in the Coast Guard Reserve, were actively patrolling coastal waters, thus releasing many a regular Coast Guardsman for other duties. Backing up the Reserve Patrol was a backlog of 300,000 boat-owners, each man familiar with some particular part of the coastline. This was one of the many innovations instituted by Vice Admiral Russell Waesche, the Coast Guard's only three-time Commandant. He now commands 175,000 men scattered over the seven seas. They man transports, have their own air force, patrol shorelines, escort convoys, and assist in the anti-submarine campaign. By far the most spectacular Coast Guard job at present is the piloting of landing craft during invasion landings. The Coast Guard was selected to train and supervise personnel for these operations because they are specialists in the handling of small craft along shore.

The present Coast Guard commander was born in the little inland village of Thurmont, Frederick County, Maryland, January 6, 1886, the son of a mining engineer. He went to public schools in Maryland and enrolled in the electrical engineering department of Purdue University. Waesche says, "I didn't have too much dough. With my brother teaching at Purdue, I figured on saving some of my board bill. After a year my brother thought I was too young to appreciate a college education and advised a little military training. Notice of the Coast Guard exam was on the bulletin board. I took it and passed. When I woke up I found I liked the service too much and was too old to get back to electrical engineering."

Admiral Waesche (pronounced Way-she) is nearly six feet tall, ruddy, sharp-eyed, and a crack marksman, especially with the rifle. He is responsible for the extensive gunnery practice now required of all Coast Guardsmen.

After Waesche was graduated from the Coast Guard Academy as an ensign on October 27, 1906, he served aboard ships in both the Atlantic and Pacific, as well as the Alaskan and Arctic Patrols. He was once shipwrecked off the bleak coast of Alaska. During the palmy days of rum-running in the 1920's Waesche was in the off-shore patrol in command of a division of destroyers.

In 1928 Waesche was detailed to Coast Guard Headquarters in Washington as Chief Ordnance Officer. Later he was made liaison officer in the War Plans Division in the Office of the Chief of Naval Operations. After this preparation Waesche became aide to the Coast Guard Commandant. Later on he was made Chief of the Finance Division.

President Roosevelt appointed Waesche Commandant of the Coast Guard in June 1936 with the rank of rear admiral. At the termination of the Commandant's four-year term, the President reappointed him to a second term, and again in May 1944, for his third four-year period. Waesche was raised to vice admiral during his second term and is the only Coast Guard Commandant to reach that rank.

During Waesche's first term as Commandant, the Lighthouse Service was made a part of the Coast Guard, thus eliminating the overlapping duties of a shore station branch and a sea-going branch.

Waesche went to work on the Coast Guard communications system as a young lieutenant. In those days phones and telegraph lines were used. The Admiral has supervised the placing of 2,500 miles of communication lines and the installation of a complete radio system. He is known as a man with ideas, solving many tough problems for the Navy. He was called in to work out new methods of air-sea rescue for postwar overseas air transport.

An executive order of the President transferred to the Coast Guard some of the duties of the Marine Inspection Bureau of the Department of Commerce. Port supervision and security was also made a part of the Coast Guard's job.

Vice Admiral Waesche has led the Coast Guard in the greatest expansion of its history under wartime conditions. The peacetime Coast Guard fleet has expanded over three times and Guardsmen man over 200 Navy vessels.

Waesche originated the Coast Guard Institute and Correspondence School for warrant officers and enlisted men and reorganized the Coast Guard field forces in 1931.

ROSTER ★ ★ ★ ★